The Mystery of the Universe and the Meaning of Human Life

Witness Lee

Living Stream Ministry
Anaheim, CA • www.lsm.org

First Edition, October 2003.

ISBN 0-7363-2416-X

Published by

Living Stream Ministry
2431 W. La Palma Ave., Anaheim, CA 92801 U.S.A.
P. O. Box 2121, Anaheim, CA 92814 U.S.A.

Printed in the United States of America

03   04   05   06   07   08   09   /   9   8   7   6   5   4   3   2   1

CONTENTS

PREFACE

This book is composed of messages given in Chinese by Brother Witness Lee from 1985 through 1990 in Taipei, Taiwan and Anaheim, California. The first seven chapters concern the gospel, Christ, and the church. The last two chapters concern the new way to meet and to serve and the functioning of every member. These messages were not reviewed by the speaker.

Chapter One

THE MYSTERY OF THE UNIVERSE

Scripture Reading: Rom. 1:19-20; Psa. 19:1; Acts 14:15-17; 17:24-28a; Job 26:7; Isa. 40:22; Gen. 1:27; 2:7a; Rom. 9:21-24a; Zech. 12:1

I. The mystery of the universe is God:
   A. "Because that which is known of God is manifest within them, for God manifested it to them. For the invisible things of Him, both His eternal power and divine characteristics, have been clearly seen since the creation of the world, being perceived by the things made, so that they would be without excuse"—Rom. 1:19-20.
   B. "The heavens declare the glory of God, / And the firmament proclaims the work of His hands"— Psa. 19:1.
   C. "The living God, who made heaven and earth and the sea and all things in them; who in the generations gone by allowed all the nations to go their ways. And yet He did not leave Himself without witness, in that He did good by giving you rain from heaven and fruitful seasons, filling your hearts with food and gladness"—Acts 14:15-17.
   D. "The God who made the world and all things in it...gives to all life and breath and all things. And He made from one every nation of men to dwell on all the face of the earth, determining beforehand their appointed seasons and the boundaries of their dwelling, that they might seek God, if perhaps they might grope for Him and find Him, even

though He is not far from each one of us; for in Him we live and move and are"—17:24-28a.

E. "He stretches out the north over the void; / He hangs the earth upon nothing"—Job 26:7.

F. "It is He who sits above the circle of the earth,... / Who stretches out the heavens like a curtain, / And spreads them out like a tent to dwell in"—Isa. 40:22.

G. The above verses prove that:

  1. God exists.

  2. God is the origin of the universe, for the heavens, the earth, and all things therein were created by Him.

  3. God is the source of mankind, for mankind was created by Him.

  4. Human beings live, move, and exist in God.

  5. God causes the heavens to give forth rain and the earth to yield produce for man's existence.

  6. The times and boundaries of all nations were determined beforehand by God.

II. God created man according to His image that man might be a vessel to contain Him:

A. "And God created man in His own image; in the image of God He created him; male and female He created them"—Gen. 1:27.

B. "Jehovah God formed man with the dust of the ground"—2:7a.

C. "Or does not the potter have authority over the clay to make out of the same lump one vessel unto honor and another unto dishonor?...God...might make known the riches of His glory upon vessels of mercy, which He had before prepared unto glory, even us, whom He has also called"—Rom. 9:21-24a.

D. "Jehovah, who stretches forth the heavens and lays the foundations of the earth and forms the spirit of man within him"—Zech. 12:1.

E. The above verses reveal that:

  1. Man was created according to God's image; God's image is expressed in His four attributes,

or characteristics: love, light, holiness, and
righteousness.

2. Man is a container created by God according to
   what He is; God wants to be man's content, and
   He wants man to be His expression.

3. Man's virtues as the outward form of God's
   attributes must have God in them as the reality
   for them to develop and shine forth.

4. Man's spirit is as important as the heavens and
   the earth; the heavens are for the earth, the
   earth is for man, and man is for God; God is
   Spirit, so God created man especially with a
   spirit as the organ to receive God.

THE BIBLE EXPLAINING ALL THE MYSTERIES
OF THE UNIVERSE

Romans 1:19 and 20 say, "Because that which is known of God is manifest within them, for God manifested it to them. For the invisible things of Him, both His eternal power and divine characteristics, have been clearly seen since the creation of the world, being perceived by the things made, so that they would be without excuse." This passage presents a profound matter and speaks forth the mysteries of the universe. In our eyes heaven, earth, and man all are mysteries. When we look at heaven, earth, and ourselves, we cannot explain them. After all, what is heaven, what is earth, and what are we human beings? Many astronomers and geologists, and some anthropologists as well, have spent much time on these questions yet have not been able to find the answers.

We have to come back to the Bible to look at these questions. It is unavoidable that throughout the centuries, scholars have been speculating in their study of heaven, earth, and man. Nevertheless, there is a book in human history called the Bible, a book written by men under divine inspiration which explains clearly the origin of heaven, earth, and man. In this Bible there is neither inference nor conjecture; rather, all is plain revelation.

The first sentence in the first book of the Bible says, "In the beginning God created the heavens and the earth" (Gen. 1:1). God said clearly that the heavens, the earth, and man were made by Him. It was only five to six hundred years ago that men discovered that the earth is round instead of flat. Therefore, they began to call the earth a globe. Yet around 700 B.C., that is, two thousand seven hundred years ago, the prophet Isaiah, one of the authors of the Old Testament, wrote in his book, saying, "It is He [God] who sits above the circle of the earth,... / Who stretches out the heavens like a curtain, / And spreads them out like a tent to dwell in" (Isa. 40:22). As far as two thousand seven hundred years back, Isaiah told people that the earth is a big circle. This proves that the origin of the heavens and the earth spoken of in the Bible is neither an inference nor a fabrication but a clear word of revelation from God.

Job 26:7 says, "He [God] stretches out the north over the void; / He hangs the earth upon nothing." Job was probably a contemporary of Abraham. Yet the book he wrote about four thousand years ago tells us that the earth is hanging upon nothing. The advance of modern day science has only proved again and again that the revelation of the Bible is totally accurate.

In the New Testament, the apostle Paul told people that the invisible things of God, both His eternal power and divine characteristics, have been clearly seen since the creation of the world, being perceived by the things made (Rom. 1:20). This means that we can know God through the heavens, the earth, and all things. For example, when we look at the numerous systems in the universe, either the solar system, the Milky Way, or others, there is no disorderliness. Up until now astronomers still cannot give us an accurate figure as to how big the universe is. This universe is truly vast. Yet after billions of years, the order of the universe is still maintained, and the solar system still revolves in perfect order. We who live on this earth can still enjoy the distinct difference between spring and summer and the definite timing of day and night.

MAN BEING GOD'S VESSEL FOR CONTAINING GOD

Just as the great things in the universe operate according to their laws, so the smaller things have their principles. We all know that there is a law, a principle, to everything, and behind all things there must be One who establishes the laws and principles. If not, where do all the laws and principles of all matters come from? The Bible clearly says that the universe was created by God. Hence, we can have a glimpse of all that God is, all that God has, God's power, and God's divine characteristics through all things in the universe. Besides, the Bible further reveals that man was created by God. Genesis 1, which is a record of God's creation of the universe, shows us how God created all things out of nothing and how He created man.

God first created the inorganic things such as the earth, the sun, air, and water. Then God created the organic things, which require air, water, the sun, and the earth. God created the different kinds of life in an orderly way, from the lower class to the highest class. He first created plants such as grass, vegetables, and trees, and then He created oviparous animals such as the fish in the sea and the birds in the air. Thereafter, He created viviparous animals such as the beasts and the cattle. At the end, God created man. Man was created in a way that is different from the other living things; God created man in His image (Gen. 1:26), and He also created a special organ for man—the human spirit—so that man may contact God. This spirit in man is the highest matter.

There is no animal among all the creatures that has the image of God or has a spirit within. Yet there is another life that is higher than the life of man, and that is the life of God Himself. God's life is the super-class life. God created man in His own image with a purpose—God's purpose is to make man His vessel. A vessel is for containing things. For example, a cup is for containing water. Likewise, as God's vessel, man is for containing God.

MAN HAVING THE CHARACTERISTIC OF DESIRING LOVE, LIGHT, HOLINESS, AND RIGHTEOUSNESS

The creation of man is an exceedingly great thing. Zechariah 12:1 says, "Jehovah, who stretches forth the heavens and lays the foundations of the earth and forms the spirit of man within him." Here the human spirit is greatly emphasized, for the verse says that at the same time that God created the heavens and the earth, He also created a spirit for man within. Man's spirit is thus as important as the heavens and the earth. This means that the heavens are for the earth to grow all things, the earth is for man's existence, and man's existence is for him to be God's vessel to express God. For this reason, when God created man, He created two things for him. One is that man has God's image without, and the other is that he has a spirit within.

The image that man possesses refers to the expression of the attributes of God. The Bible tells us that God's attributes are love, light, holiness, and righteousness. These can be clearly seen from the Ten Commandments in the Old Testament. We all know that a certain kind of a person will enact a certain kind of law. Good people enact good laws, while bad people enact bad laws. The Ten Commandments enacted by God make manifest what kind of God He is. The essence of the Ten Commandments is simply love, light, holiness, and righteousness. These four virtues are God's divine characteristics.

The Bible tells us over and over again that God is light (1 John 1:5), God is love (4:8), God is holy (1 Pet. 1:15-16), and God is righteous (Exo. 9:27). God is light, and in Him is no darkness at all. God is love, and He loves the world. God is holy, and in Him is no filthiness. God is righteous; in Him is total justice and impartiality, without any crookedness at all. The emphasis of His Ten Commandments is that we should have love, light, holiness, and righteousness. Since we were created according to God's image, even though we became fallen and corrupted, to this day we still have these four elements in us.

We appreciate kindness. When we love people and treat them benevolently, we feel comfortable within. But if we cheat or hate people, we feel unspeakably miserable. This shows that there is love in man. Moreover, everyone has a predisposition for light. If a person does evil, he deeply reproaches himself within and does not need others to rebuke him. Not only so, no one likes to do filthy things; rather, everyone hopes to be upright and have a just heart. The Chinese always say, "Justice is in man's heart." All this tells us that when man was created, he was created according to God's image of love, light, holiness, and righteousness. Within man there is the predisposition, or desire, for these four virtues, and this predisposition is not out of man himself but was created for man by God.

When we observe other creatures, we discover that among the animals, whether cows, sheep, cats, dogs, horses, or donkeys, none of them possesses these four virtues nor has any feeling or tendency toward them. This is because the animals were not created in God's image. Only man was created in God's image of love, light, holiness, and righteousness; therefore, within man are the characteristics of these four virtues.

GOD BEING MAN'S CONTENT,
AND MAN BEING GOD'S EXPRESSION

Even though man has the characteristics of love, light, holiness, and righteousness within, he has only the image but not the reality of love, light, holiness, and righteousness. For example, we wear gloves in cold winters. A pair of gloves has ten fingers like the hands, but that is only a pair of gloves, not the hands themselves. The gloves have been created for the hands; therefore, there must be the hands inside the gloves for the reality to be there. The gloves are empty and floppy without the hands. This is why man always feels empty. Man was not created for himself; rather, he was created to be God's vessel to contain God. If man does not contain God, he is empty, weak, and without reality like a pair of gloves.

Today man feels empty, insecure, wavering, and restless and has no calming and stabilizing power within, simply because he lacks God within. God is man's content, and man should be God's expression. For this goal, God created a spirit especially for man. This spirit is the organ for man to contact God, just like the receiver in a radio. Even though a radio may have all the outward parts, if there is no receiver, or if the receiver is out of order, this radio cannot function. Regardless of how hard you try to tune to the right frequency, you will not be able to receive the radio waves in the air. Our heart is like a radio, and our spirit is that receiver; if we turn our spirit to focus on God, we can touch Him.

A great part of the human spirit is the conscience, which is man's deepest part. In your mind perhaps you have never thought about the existence of God, and you have never seen God with your eyes. However, your conscience, the deep part in you, your spirit, always gives you a feeling that there is a Supreme Being, that there is a God in this universe. This proves two things. First, you have a spirit within, and second, you need God in your spirit.

MAN HAVING REAL SATISFACTION
ONLY WHEN GOD AS THE SPIRIT
ENTERS INTO MAN'S SPIRIT

God loves us and has created a stomach for us in our body

that we may take in food. Outside of us, God has prepared for us all kinds of food, including the supply from plants, the supply from animals, and the supply from minerals. God supplies man not only with food but also with drink. Besides these provisions that are necessary for man's physical existence, something that is more precious within man is the human spirit. God created man with a spirit for man to receive Him.

The gospel we preach today is not merely to tell people that they are sinful and must therefore believe in Jesus to avoid perdition. Rather, we tell people that the universe is a sphere created by God for Himself, that in it He could create man as a vessel in which He can put Himself. Every human being, whoever he is, whether male or female, old or young, as soon as he approaches twenty years of age, deep in him there is an inexplicable question, "What is the purpose of my life? What is the meaning of the human life? Where do the heavens and the earth come from? What is the universe all about?" Actually, not only is this universe a mystery, but God also is a mystery, and even we ourselves are a mystery.

Once I was invited to have supper with a group of doctors. One of them, a non-Christian, said to me, "We who are students of medical science, after dissecting a corpse, cannot help but bow down our heads to confess that there is a Creator in this universe, because the human body is structured so wonderfully." This word is true. Even for one like me who does not know medical science or any other science, I am amazed whenever I look at myself in the mirror. The ears are facing the front and are shaped like an arc, resembling receivers. If the ears faced the back and were not shaped like an arc, we would find it difficult to hear any sound. Furthermore, our nose facing down meets our exact need. If our nose faced up, dust and rain water would get into the nostrils. Who has arranged and designed this for man? Not only so, but man is truly a wonderful living creature with thoughts and wisdom, being able to produce a spacecraft to land on the moon. Are all these coincidences? Without a doubt, all these have been designed and created by the Supreme Being in the universe.

All those who study science, physics, and medicine ultimately say that there must be a Sovereign One in the universe. Concerning this point, the Bible says clearly what heaven is, what the earth is, and what man is. The Bible even tells us what God Himself is. John 4:24 says, "God is Spirit." Man has a spirit, and God is spirit. Man is God's vessel, and the pneumatic God wants to enter into man to be his content to satisfy him. In other words, since man is a vessel created by God, without God, man can never be satisfied. This is the same as the human stomach, which is for containing food. Without food, the stomach will definitely feel hungry, uncomfortable, and unsatisfied.

Take the example of one from a humble origin who finally becomes successful after many years of hard work. He is successful in his career and is respected by others. He does not have to worry about his daily necessities, and you may say that he has enjoyed all honor and fame. Both in his physical and psychological needs, he has a way to attain to the highest and best level. Yet at this juncture he discovers that he has a lack in the depth of his being. Within him he has a very deep thirst which cannot be satisfied by material things and amusements. This is the real situation of man. Even though there is a difference in degree concerning our outward material life, there rises up in the deepest part of every man's heart an inexplicable sigh. Without God, man is in a state of emptiness.

MAN NEEDING GOD TO BE
THE STABILIZING POWER IN HIS LIFE

Human beings, regardless of race or skin color, have the need to worship God. Of all the living creatures, only man feels the need of worshipping God. We have never seen a cow or a horse erect a small temple to worship God; neither have we seen a cat or a dove setting up something as a symbol of God for worship. Nevertheless, the concept of worshipping God is very common among the human race. Even the least civilized aborigines set up a bonfire to worship as god. From this we can see that the human heart desperately desires to find the true God who created the universe and all things in it. There is a story of someone whose heart was hardened and who did not believe in God, yet at his deathbed, when he was asked if he needed anything, he replied that he wanted a Bible.

Though man may deny the existence of God in broad daylight, in the deep of the night, in solitude and quietness, when he examines himself, he worries as to what he should do if there really is God. This tells us that man was created by God and that he was even created for God. Therefore, man needs God. Hundreds of thousands of Christians can bear the same testimony that their human life had been empty for more than half of their life until they met Jesus and called on His name and that they became satisfied within because of Him.

Many friends who have not yet believed in the Lord wonder why Christians seem to have something extra, something as a "motor" in them. Some Christians previously spoke little, yet after they believed in Jesus, they try their best to preach Jesus to others. Not just one or two but nearly all of them are like this. This is because the believers of Jesus have tasted the sweetness of the Lord, and they have obtained real satisfaction and rest. Previously their human life was like a big boat tossing in the sea, without any stabilizing power within. But now that they have gained Jesus as their Savior and therefore have a stabilizing power, how can they refrain from preaching to others?

Our human life is like a boat in the sea, and there is the real need of a stabilizing power. This stabilizing power is the God who has created us. He is waiting to enter into us. Once God enters into us, He can satisfy our heart and remove our sense of vanity and despair. May the Spirit of God operate in each one of us that we may gain Him as the Savior of our life.

(A message given on December 6, 1985 at a gospel meeting in Taipei.)

CHAPTER TWO

THE MEANING OF HUMAN LIFE

Scripture Reading: Eph. 2:12; John 7:37-38; 6:35; 14:6; 10:10;
1 John 5:12a; Col. 3:4; Gal. 2:20a; Phil. 1:20b-21a

I. The meaning of human life is Christ:
   A. "Apart from Christ,…having no hope and without God in the world"—Eph. 2:12.
   B. "Jesus stood and cried out, saying, If anyone thirsts, let him come to Me and drink. He who believes into Me, as the Scripture said, out of his innermost being shall flow rivers of living water"—John 7:37-38.
   C. "Jesus said to them, I am the bread of life; he who comes to Me shall by no means hunger, and he who believes into Me shall by no means ever thirst"—6:35.
   D. The above verses show that:
      1. Human life apart from Christ is without God and therefore without hope or goal.
      2. Human life is meaningless without Christ.
II. Christ wants to be man's life:
   A. "Jesus said…I am…the life"—14:6.
   B. "I [Christ] have come that they [men] may have life and may have it abundantly"—10:10.
   C. "He who has the Son has the life"—1 John 5:12a.
   D. The verses above reveal that:
      1. Man's life being an empty vessel must have Christ as its content.
      2. Christ wants to be man's life so that the human life can be enriched and become meaningful.

III. Christ is the life of those who believe in Him:
   A. "Christ our life"—Col. 3:4.
   B. "It is no longer I who live, but it is Christ who lives in me"—Gal. 2:20a.
   C. "For to me, to live is Christ"—Phil. 1:21a.
   D. "Even now Christ will be magnified in my body, whether through life or through death"—v. 20b.
   E. The above verses describe:
      1. How Christ becomes the life of those who believe in Him.
      2. How believers of Christ live out Christ and take Him as the goal of glory.

Prayer: Lord Jesus, we worship You as the Lord of the heavens and the earth. We offer our thanks and praise to You that we can be here enjoying peace and freedom and that we have such a good opportunity to preach Your gospel. When we are preaching the gospel, we ask that You remember our country, the head of our country, and all the government officials. May the Lord bless them and give them health, wisdom, and understanding that they can govern this country. We ask You further to grant Your visitation to all the people of this country so that they can hear the gospel. We pray that within these five years Taiwan can be gospelized, that everyone will hear the gospel, and that everywhere there will be Your testimony. Lord, may You bless each one. May Your Spirit that penetrates everywhere and gives grace abundantly operate in many ways and in every corner, reaching each one's spirit, touching each one's emotion, and opening each one's understanding so that each one will turn his heart to You and receive You as his Savior.

O Lord, we are all sinful people who desire to receive grace in Your sight. We want to repent to You and confess our sins. We believe that You are in our mouth and in our heart. When we open our mouth to call on You, You will enter into us to be our Savior, our sins will be forgiven, and we will be accepted by God and fully have peace with You. Lord, we say again to You that You are our Lord and our God. We believe in You, we love You, and we follow You. In Your precious name we pray. Amen.

MAN HAVING GOD'S IMAGE WITHOUT
AND A SPIRIT WITHIN

There are a few verses here that can be considered as the sweetest and richest in life in the whole of the Scripture. The first portion is Ephesians 2:12: "You were at that time apart from Christ,...having no hope and without God in the world." This tells us that as those who live in the world, there is no hope if we are apart from Christ, because we do not have God. God created the universe with a purpose, and for this purpose He created man. God created man differently than He did all other things. First, He created man according to His own image. As He Himself is love, light, holiness, and righteousness, so He put these virtues into man. Therefore, when a person is born, inherently he has love, light, holiness, and righteousness. From the depths of our being, we all hope to be persons of love, light, holiness, and righteousness. Yet all these are only the outward form. Consider the example of a glove: it has just the outward form of the hand. Only when a hand is inserted can there be the reality of the glove.

Since God wants to enter into us to be our life and reality, God has created a spirit for man within. This has been especially created by God for each one. This spirit within man is like the receiver of a radio and is able to receive the "sound waves" from the heavens. Yes, we all have God's image, but that is only outward. Now within us there is an organ which can receive God. That organ is our spirit. Therefore, if we do not open our heart to let this God come in, as far as we ourselves are concerned, we are only an empty shell, an empty vessel. We need to receive God into our spirit to be our content.

HUMAN LIFE WITHOUT CHRIST
BEING UTTERLY HOPELESS

Throughout human history there have been tens of thousands of books, yet it is a marvelous thing that from the past to the present only one book is called the Holy Bible, the Holy Book. This book is indeed holy for it is God's speaking and God's breathing out (2 Tim. 3:16). This book tells us from the very start that "in the beginning God created the heavens and the earth" (Gen. 1:1). We do not need to speculate, for it clearly tells us that God created the heavens and the earth. Even modern science has proved that God indeed used the dust of the earth to create man, because the elements found in man are compatible with those found in the dust of the earth. God first created our body, and then He created a spirit for us that we may contain Him.

However, the spirit of man lost its function due to man's fall, so God came to be a man and died for us on the cross as our Savior. When He resurrected from the dead, He became the ever-living Spirit, not only forgiving our sins but also entering into us to be our life. What a sweet salvation! What a wonderful fact! The Lord who created the universe, the God of all, is actually willing to enter into us, who were created yet fallen people, to be our life. This is indeed a great matter in the universe. For this reason, the Bible tells us that if we live apart from this Christ, our human life is without hope. Why is it without hope? It is because we are without God.

The Christ in whom we believe is God Himself. He was God who came to be among men, and He was God manifesting Himself to man, that is, God reaching man. This God who has reached us is our Savior. Once we receive Him, He and we have a spiritual union in life. He enters into us, and we enter into Him. Therefore, if our human life is without Christ and God, we are truly without a goal. The hope previously mentioned refers to this goal.

When we are endeavoring for our career, living a very busy life, we may not feel as much the pain of having no hope. However, when we have achieved success and have acquired fame, and when we have obtained all that we desire to have, we will sense a great lack and a great dissatisfaction in the depths of our being. We cannot say for sure where the shortage is, but we do experience it. Particularly before graduation from college we readily feel the vanity and emptiness of human life. What will our future be? What is the direction of our human life? This tells us that without God and Christ, our human life has no goal. A human life without a goal is the greatest reason for our feeling of vanity. If a person does not have God in his spirit, no matter how prosperous his career is, how numerous his achievements are, or how high his position is, he will still have a great sense of emptiness and dissatisfaction.

GOD AS WATER, AIR, AND FOOD TO MAN

Once when the Lord Jesus was on the earth, on the last day of a feast, He stood up among a crowd and cried out, "If anyone thirsts, let him come to Me and drink" (John 7:37). Why did He wait until the last day of the feast to stand up and speak this word? This is because it was on the last day of the feast, after the people had rejoiced a few days and were about to go away, that the sense of emptiness came. At that juncture, Jesus stood up and cried, "He who believes into

Me...out of his innermost being shall flow rivers of living water" (v. 38). The "living water" and the "innermost being" mentioned here are both figures of speech, pointing to the fact that this Savior as the Spirit of life wants to enter into us as living water to quench the thirst of us who thirst.

Not only so, but today our Lord is also "breath." After His death and resurrection, He returned to be among the disciples, breathed into them, and said to them, "Receive the Holy Spirit" (20:22). The Greek word for *spirit* is the same as that for *breath*. Therefore, here this can be translated as, "Receive the Holy Breath." Our Lord, our God, is to us like air. Today all things exist altogether by depending on this breath of life. If there were no air, all living things could not live. Air is only a sign, whereas the Lord Jesus is the reality. He is the real air. The Lord wants to come into us. As the real life, He comes into us to solve the problem of our inward vanity. Our human life has hope only when we are filled with Christ within.

The Lord Jesus is not only our water of life to quench our thirst. He is not only the real breath of life coming into us to take away our emptiness. He is also our bread of life so that we who eat Him shall by no means ever hunger. When the Lord Jesus was on earth, He said to people, "I am the bread of life; he who comes to Me shall by no means hunger, and he who believes into Me shall by no means ever thirst" (6:35). In human history no writer of any book has ever dared to speak in such a way. Who could speak such words as, "If anyone thirsts, let him come to Me and drink"; "he who believes into Me...out of his innermost being shall flow rivers of living water"; and "I am the bread of life; he who comes to Me shall by no means hunger, and he who believes into Me shall by no means ever thirst"? Only the God who created the universe can speak such words.

JESUS DESIRING TO GIVE ETERNAL LIFE
TO THOSE WHO BELIEVE

This God who created the universe and all things wants to be our bread of life and water of life. No matter whether our sense of human life is hunger or thirst, He can solve the problem for us. If we are hungry, He is our bread of life; if we are thirsty, He is our water of life. After saying that He is the bread of life and the water of life, one day He again spoke a very mysterious word. He said, "I am...the life" (John 11:25). In Greek, there are three different words denoting life: *bios* (Luke 8:14), referring to our visible, physical life; *psuche* (Matt. 16:25-26; John 12:25), referring to our soul-life; and *zoe* (Eph. 4:18; 1 John 1:2; Heb. 7:16), referring to God's life, the spiritual life. The Lord Jesus said, "I am the life." This life is neither bios nor psuche but *zoe*.

In other words, the Lord Jesus wants to be our life—not our *bios* life nor our *psuche* life but our *zoe* life. God desires to be our life, a life we do not have in ourselves. We have a physical life in the flesh and a soulish life as well, but we do not have the eternal, divine life of God. This divine life is what we need, and it is also what is indispensable for us. If we live by our created life in the flesh, we will not be satisfied, and our human life will be without a goal and without hope. This is because both our physical life and our soulish life are temporary and corruptible, not eternal.

Only God's *zoe,* the divine life, is the eternal life. Some Bible versions translate *eternal life* as *everlasting life.* John 3:36a says, "He who believes into the Son has eternal life." This means that those who believe into Christ have eternal life. The Lord Jesus said this word to prove His greatness, because in all of the sacred words spoken on earth, all that man can boast of is good doctrine, good teaching, and good philosophy. No man has ever said that he is life. No man is qualified to say this word except the Lord Jesus. The Lord Jesus can say so because He is life. He is the eternal life.

THE LORD CAUSING THOSE WHO RECEIVE HIM TO HAVE LIFE ABUNDANTLY

The Lord Jesus said in John 10:10, "I have come that they [men] may have life and may have it abundantly." The Lord Jesus has come that man may not only have life but may have it more abundantly. How does the Lord Jesus cause us to have His life? The Bible tells us that He became flesh, passed through human living, and eventually went to die on the cross with our sins, thereby dealing with all of them. He died for our sins, was buried, and three days later He resurrected from the dead. Throughout human history, there has never been any leader or founder of a religion that has resurrected from the dead. Jesus Christ is the only One who died and resurrected.

Once He resurrected, He became the life-giving Spirit (1 Cor. 15:45b). Today He is on the throne in the heavens as the Lord of all. However, because He is the all-penetrating Spirit, He can be believed in and received by man by reaching man as "air." This is the way He gives us life. For over fifty years I have been learning to work for the Lord, and I have traveled to a number of places where I have heard many testimonies of how people believed in the Lord. All those testimonies were nearly the same. The believers of the Lord Jesus all testified that before they met the Lord, their human living had been mostly empty and miserable. Nevertheless, after they received the Lord Jesus, and after He entered into them, their lives underwent a tremendous change.

Once a friend who worked in the customs office said to me, "Your words have solved my problem. I would like to believe in Jesus, but I do not know the way. Please tell me how to receive the Lord Jesus." I said to him, "This God who is the Lord of the heavens and the earth became a man and died for us on the cross. Moreover, He resurrected from the dead and became the life-giving Spirit. Today He is in the heavens and on the earth. He is in every place where we are. That is why Romans 10:8 says that 'the word is near you, in your mouth and in your heart.' After you return home, find a quiet place to call on Him and say to Him, 'Lord Jesus, You are my Savior, I confess my sins to You.' Whatever feeling the Lord gives you concerning your sins, confess accordingly. When you pray to the Lord in this way, surely something will happen."

This friend told me later that after hearing my word, he went back to pray to the Lord. The next day when he went to work, his colleagues were greatly surprised when they saw that he did not smoke as he usually did. Because he had believed in Jesus he spontaneously quit smoking. Not only so, he used to be a person who liked to tell jokes and make fun of others, but after believing in Jesus, he was delivered from all the outward pleasures of the flesh. Later his whole family also believed in Jesus. A few years later even the colleagues who lived in his neighborhood all believed in Jesus, household by household.

GOD'S LIFE ENTERING INTO MAN AND BEING EXPRESSED THROUGH MAN

One time after preaching the gospel, a judge came and said to me, "I want to receive the Savior whom you preached. But I do not know how." I said the same thing to him. I asked him to find a quiet place to call on the name of the Lord Jesus, and he did as I said. The next morning when he was on his way to the court, he suddenly felt that the heavens and the earth had changed their color. He could not help but laugh. As he arrived at his office, his colleagues noticed that he was different from before in that he had a smiling face, and they asked him, "What happened to you? Did you win the lottery?" He could not explain but just kept smiling. When he returned home, his wife saw him and asked, "What is the matter with you?" He felt that he seemed to have become another person. He truly had an unspeakable joy within. Not long afterward he quit his job as a judge and became a preacher to share with others the life that he had obtained.

I give you these two examples to show you that our human life is for God. The purpose of our existence is to receive God into us as life. Only in this way will we no longer sense the vanity of human life. In the New Testament there is an apostle named Paul, who said in Colossians 3:4 that Christ is our life. He also said in Galatians 2:20, "It is no longer I who live, but it is Christ who lives in me." Not only so, he said in Philippians 1:20b and 21a, "As always, even now Christ will be magnified in my body, whether through life or through death. For to me, to live is Christ." These words seem puzzling and hard to comprehend. How can it be that for us to live is Christ? Yet in nature, God has arranged something—grafting—to illustrate this.

We all know that in botany, grafting means to unite two trees. A farmer grafts a branch of a sweet tree into that of a sour tree so that the life of the sweet tree can enter into the sour tree and the life of the sour tree can enter into the sweet tree. Eventually these two lives are joined together to become one life. The fruit produced thereafter is the expression of the sweet tree through the sour tree. To the sour tree, the sweet tree is its life, so it is no longer the sour tree that lives, but it is the sweet tree that lives in it. If the sour tree could speak, it would declare, "As always, even now the sweet tree will be magnified in my body, whether through wind and frost or through rain and snow." This is the life of a Christian.

This is not a shallow gospel. This is the mysterious yet simple truth in the Bible. All you need to do is open your heart and call on His name, telling him, "Lord Jesus, I believe in You. I want to receive You." In this way you can obtain this ever-living Savior of the universe, and He will be in you to be your life.

(A message given on December 7, 1985 at a gospel meeting in Taipei.)

CHAPTER THREE

CHRIST LIVES IN ME

Scripture Reading: Col. 2:2; 1:27; 1 Tim. 3:16; Gal. 2:20

RECEIVING THE BURDEN
TO TAKE CARE OF THE NEWLY SAVED SAINTS

From August and September of 1986, when we started the Full-time Training in Taipei, the total number of people who have been led to the Lord and baptized through door-knocking has reached more than 17,500. Therefore, we beseech the brothers and sisters to receive a burden from the Lord to take care of these new ones and to pray much for this matter.

THE CENTRAL MYSTERY OF THE BIBLE—CHRIST

We hope to help all the newly baptized brothers and sisters to see the central mystery in the Bible. Through several thousand years of testing, the Bible has been recognized as the book of books. It is the most noble and excellent book in many aspects, such as literature, truth, and ethics. The Bible does not merely teach us to know God and to worship God, nor does it teach us merely how to live and walk in an excelling way. Rather, in a deeper way it unveils to us many mysteries. These mysteries include the mystery of God, the mystery of the universe, the mystery of human life, the mystery of the kingdom of the heavens, the mystery of Christ, the mystery of the church, the mystery of life, the mystery of resurrection, the transformation and rapture of the believers, the consummation of the age, the millennial kingdom, and eternity. Of these, the mystery of Christ and the mystery of the church are great and deep, and all these mysteries are unfathomable.

First, we want to see the mystery of Christ. Christ is not merely a character in history. He is a person who transcends history. He is so unfathomable that it is very hard for man to know Him thoroughly. Throughout the generations, historians have been studying to find out who this Christ is. Even when Jesus was on earth, many were studying Him and asking, "Who then is this?" (Mark 4:41; Luke 8:25; cf. Matt. 21:10; Luke 7:49; 9:9). He Himself asked His disciples, "But you, who do you say that I am?" (Matt. 16:15). He is too profound and too all-inclusive; moreover, He is the One who fills all in all. Therefore, it is not a simple matter to understand Him.

According to the Bible, there are over three hundred items concerning the person of Christ. Here, we will briefly bring out twelve items. First, Christ is the only true God in the universe. There is no other God besides Him (1 Cor. 8:4; Rom. 9:5). Second, He is the Creator of the universe, including the heavens, the earth, and all things (Heb. 1:10). All things did not come out of evolution; rather, they came into existence through the Lord's creation. Third, He is the Upholder of the universe; as such, He upholds and bears all things so that the whole universe can operate orderly (1:3). Fourth, He is the Lord, the Possessor, of the universe, and all things belong to Him (Acts 2:36; 10:36). Fifth, He is God yet man; He is God putting on human flesh and taking on humanity to be a real man (John 1:1, 14; 1 Tim. 3:16). Sixth, as God yet man He lived thirty-three and a half years on earth (Phil. 2:7-8a; Heb. 2:17-18; 4:15). Seventh, as the Redeemer He bore our sins on the cross and died and bled for us to accomplish redemption (1 Pet. 2:24a; John 19:34; Eph. 1:7).

Eighth, He is the life-giving Spirit (1 Cor. 15:45b). After He died and was buried, because He had the divine, eternal, and uncreated life in Him, He resurrected from the dead and became the life-giving Spirit to impart Himself to us as life. Ninth, as our Savior He applies salvation to us in all our circumstances and environments (Luke 2:11; Phil. 1:19). Tenth, as our good Shepherd He shepherds us and takes care of us (John 10:11). Eleventh, as the High Priest appointed by God, He prays for us before God and bears all our problems (Heb.

2:17-18; 4:15). Twelfth, He is the King established by God to be the King of kings. Only He is the highest King in the universe (Rev. 1:5; 19:16).

THE MYSTERIOUS CHRIST
BEING TRANSCENDENT AND TRUSTWORTHY

First of all, this mysterious Christ has a moral standard that is transcendent. Especially in the record of the Gospel of Luke, where the details of Christ's living are depicted, we can see that His speech, His character, and His moral standard were all transcendent. For example, He required people not only to love others but also to love their enemies (6:27). He required people not only to be clean and pure in their outward behavior but also to be pure in their inward motive (cf. 11:39-41). Therefore, His moral standard was transcendent.

Second, His words were trustworthy. He never said anything far-fetched, like the things found in myths. Third, His wisdom was extraordinary. He formed many of the extraordinary expressions in the Bible. For example, He said that He is the life and the bread of life as well, and that he who comes to Him shall by no means hunger (John 6:35); that He has the water of life, and he who draws near to Him shall by no means thirst forever (4:14); that He is the resurrection (11:25); and that He is God Himself (1:1, 14). These words which otherwise might sound proud and haughty contain a great deal of wisdom and cannot be spoken by ordinary people. That is why Rousseau, a writer and a philosopher in France, said that if the Bible were a fabrication, the one who fabricated it would be the greatest inventor. Christ is truly a trustworthy One. His moral standard is transcendent, and His wisdom is extraordinary, yet His living was very practical. Whatever He said is practical and has reality.

Furthermore, few great men prophesied concerning the things in the future. Only Jesus Christ prophesied concerning the things that would happen on earth and the things that would be accomplished in the future after His departure. All those who study history have been surprised that two thousand years ago, during the time of Christ when the modern world situation was yet to be formed, He already told us all about the world situation in principle. To put it briefly, according to Matthew 24, after the resurrection and ascension of the Lord, the first thing to happen on the earth was that the gospel was to be preached to the whole inhabited earth (v. 14). Today, among the five great religions in the world, not one of them has been preached as widely as Christianity. The Bible has been translated into almost all languages and dialects. Nearly every place inhabited by men has the preaching of the gospel and the translation of the Bible.

Along with the spreading of the gospel, wars were to become rampant, and nation was to rise up against nation, and kingdom against kingdom (v. 7a). In these two thousand years, wars on the earth have increased constantly. The Bible also says that earthquakes were to be intensified constantly (v. 7b). Geologists all acknowledge that there have never been so many earthquakes in these two thousand years as there have been in the recent days. All these prophecies prove that Jesus Christ is the extraordinary One. He is God, and the prophecies He spoke have already been fulfilled for the most part. This shows that His words are trustworthy.

CHRIST BEING LIFE IN OUR SPIRIT

This Christ who is transcendent and trustworthy now lives in us to be our subjective experience. Christ is the all-inclusive One, yet He lives in us. Therefore, we have to realize that even though the Bible teaches us how to conduct ourselves as human beings, this is not the center of the Bible. The center of the Bible is this wonderful, extraordinary Christ. He is both God and man, and He is all-inclusive. He created the universe (Gen. 1:1), became flesh (John 1:14), went to the cross to bear the sins of and die for the whole human race (1 Pet. 2:24), and in His resurrection He became the life-giving Spirit (1 Cor. 15:45b) to enter into us to be our life (John 20:22; Col. 3:4).

He came into man as life, not by the touching of the human hand, nor by the seeing of the human eye, nor by the hearing of the human ear, but by the spirit in the depths of man echoing to God as the Spirit. The spirit, in the deepest part of man, is the place where man can sense the Spirit of

God (John 4:24; Rom. 8:14-16). Only through His becoming flesh, going to the cross to die, and becoming the life-giving Spirit can He enter into man to dispense life. Therefore, after we believe in the Lord and are saved, the divine life is added into us. This is different from all religions. All those who believe in the Lord Jesus in truthfulness feel that something has been added into them after they have called on His name sincerely (Rom. 10:9-13). Actually, what has been added into them is a person—Christ as the Spirit living in them.

THE GOD WHO IS LOVE, LIGHT, HOLINESS, AND RIGHTEOUSNESS LIVING IN US TO MAKE US LIKE HIM

The primary work of the Lord who lives in us is to transform us completely with His life and nature. God's life and nature mainly lie in God's love, light, holiness, and righteousness. In other words, God is a God of love, light, holiness, and righteousness. These four points include all the ethics, morality, and proper behavior among men. No matter what nation it is, all its laws are within the boundary of these four words.

Love is God's essence (1 John 4:8, 16), light is God's expression (1:5), holiness is God's nature (1 Pet. 1:15-16), and righteousness is God's procedure (Psa. 89:14; Rom. 14:17; 1:17; 1 John 1:9; 2:29). That God is holy means that He is different from all that is common. He is without defilement and without mixture; indeed, He is a God who is simple and pure. To be righteous is to be just and upright, without crookedness. Hence, God being righteousness indicates that everything of God is proper. Such a God who is love, light, holiness, and righteousness is the Lord Jesus Himself. When He enters into us to be our life, He works these attributes and virtues into us.

Some saints have been saved for only a few months, but they can testify that in them there is One who supplies them all the time and who also regulates them according to God's love, light, holiness, and righteousness. After we receive the Lord Jesus and are saved, if there is anything that contradicts love, light, holiness, and righteousness in the way we

conduct ourselves and in our daily life, He will give us a feeling within, causing us to have no peace. The feeling brought
to us by God's operating in us is the indisputable proof that
He lives in us. The feeling that He gives man within is gentle
and fine, just like a dove which is gentle and guileless (John
1:32). Not only so, He is in us as a living person, not merely a
kind of feeling.

Before we believed in the Lord Jesus, sometimes we had a
feeling of doing good, and sometimes we also had a feeling of
sinfulness. Yet those feelings were never very deep and heavy.
God shows us that He Himself is love, light, holiness, and
righteousness. Therefore, the way we conduct ourselves must
also be love, light, holiness, and righteousness. As long as we
have this kind of feeling within, it proves that Jesus Christ
lives in us. His living in us includes His operating, moving,
and acting. Even though Jesus Christ in us is meek and
tender, He is not quiet and stationary. Rather, He is acting all
the time, and His actions are very gentle. Sometimes, we do
not feel His existence, but we actually have Someone within
regulating us all the time.

If we conduct ourselves by the inner regulation, the issue
of our conduct will be a living that is like God. God is love, so
what we live out is also love. God is light, so what we live out
is also light. God is holiness, so how we act and what we do is
according to holiness. God is righteousness, so we are proper
and righteous in all the ways that we conduct ourselves and
in our contact with people. The fact that we can live out such
conditions proves that we are submitting ourselves to the
Christ who lives within us.

COOPERATING WITH CHRIST AND OBEYING HIM

Christ lives in us, and what He needs is that we cooperate
with Him. Therefore, Romans 12:1 says that after we have
been saved, we should present ourselves to God. To present
ourselves to God means to tell Him, "O Lord, You are living in
me, and I want to cooperate with You by giving myself to You
to listen to You and to obey You. Whatever You do in me to
regulate me, lead me, and touch me, I will do accordingly and

obey." This obedience will cause us to be saved by Him from day to day and moment by moment.

CONTACTING THE LORD
IN SPIRIT THROUGH PRAYER

God as Spirit lives in our spirit. We use our eyes to see, our ears to hear, our nose to smell, our mouth to eat, and our stomach to digest food. In the same manner, today God is Spirit, so for us to contact Him we have to use our spirit. The way to use the spirit is to pray. The more we pray to contact this pneumatic Christ, the better. We should not pray according to the imagination of our mind. Rather, we should pray according to the depths of our being, a part that is deeper than our mind. This means that we should pray by our spirit. When we pray by the spirit deep within, we feel that we have touched the Lord in the spirit. Therefore, when we pray, we may close our eyes to avoid being distracted by things outside. When we close our eyes, not letting things from the outside get into us, we can tell our feeling to the Lord with words from the depths of our being. The more we pray in this way, the more we contact the Lord. The more we pray, the more our spirit is filled with His Spirit. If we pray more, we will have more feelings within. If we pray weightily, we will feel weighty within. If we pray deeply, we will feel deep within.

We hope that the saints can practice this word and spend more time to pray before the Lord to contact the Lord Himself. The Lord is already in us, so the more we pray, the more we allow Him to increase in us, have more ground in us, and spread more in us. The more we allow Him to regulate us with His love, light, holiness, and righteousness, the more we receive grace and are filled by Him in order to spontaneously live out a living that is greatly different from our former way of living. In the past we lived alone. Now Christ is lived out of us so that we may live a God-like living, that is, a living of love, light, holiness, and righteousness. Only in this way can we be spiritual, sanctified, victorious, and able to grow in life. Therefore, a Christian is one who has Christ living within and who lets Christ live in him. The Christian life is a life that allows Christ to live out through us to express God's love, light, holiness, and righteousness.

(A message given on March 15, 1987 at a conference in Taipei.)

CHAPTER FOUR

CHRIST BEING THE CONTENT AND REALITY OF ALL VIRTUES

EXPERIENCING CHRIST AS OUR VIRTUES

Philippians, a book concerning the experience of Christ, was written by the apostle Paul, who was full of the experience of Christ. Paul said in chapter one that Christ would be magnified as always in his body, whether through life or through death (v. 20), and he went on to say that for him to live was Christ (v. 21). Christ was his inward life and also his outward expression. In chapter two he spoke about how he took Christ as his pattern (vv. 5-11). In chapter three he explained how he himself regarded Christ as the One of supreme preciousness and how he even suffered the loss of all things and counted them as refuse that he might gain, enjoy, and experience Christ (v. 8). At the end, in the last chapter, he charged and exhorted us with six virtues (4:8). Now we want to see in a practical way the six items in which we experience Christ as our virtues.

SIX VIRTUES IN PHILIPPIANS CHAPTER FOUR

In Philippians 4 Paul referred to six virtues: being true, being dignified, being righteous, being pure, being lovely, and being well spoken of. What is described here is very beautiful. To be true is to be without falsehood, without lying, and without vanity, to be real and truthful in everything. To be dignified is to be venerable, noble, grave, and able to fully inspire and invite reverence. To be righteous is to be without anything that is wrong and to be right before God and man. To be pure is to be single, without any mixture. To be lovely is to be agreeable and endearing. To be well spoken of is to be of good repute and to be winning.

These six items stressed by Paul are superior to what most people refer to as "truth, goodness, and beauty." These six items are divided into three groups: truthfulness and dignity, rightness and purity, and loveliness and being well spoken of. The Greek word for *virtue* spoken of by Paul in 4:8 denotes any virtue expressed through the development of the inner life. Such virtues are not produced by outward efforts; rather, they are manifested through the development of the inner life. This may be likened to the fruit borne by a tree. The fruit is not something as an outward ornamentation or decoration. It is the issue of the development of the tree's life. The virtues we speak of are the good fruits produced from the development of the inner life. Verse 8 says, "If there is any virtue and if any praise." First there is a kind of virtue as the expression of the inner nature, and then these virtues win people's praise.

THE EXPERIENCE OF CHRIST ISSUING IN
THE EXPRESSION OF VIRTUES

The apostle Paul was a person who experienced Christ, and the virtues which he mentioned that should be found in our human living are not worked out by ourselves. If we look at the context of this book, these virtues are produced as the expression of letting Christ live in us. Paul said that regardless of the circumstances, whether through life or through death, he would always let Christ be magnified in his body, for to him, to live was Christ (1:20-21). Since he lived Christ and expressed Christ, such virtues as truthfulness, dignity, righteousness, purity, loveliness, and being well spoken of were produced. All these virtues were developed out of the inner life and were fully worthy of praise. Our goal as Christians is to live out such virtues by living and expressing Christ.

We bring people to Christ not to improve their lives or reform their conduct, but to cause them to have the life of God so that they can live out and express God. The Bible reveals that God Himself is the One who is true, dignified, righteous, pure, lovely, and well spoken of. He is worthy of our praise and reverence. He created man so that man may express Him that He may be glorified in man. For this cause, He created man in His image (Gen. 1:26), which is love, light, holiness, and righteousness. When love, light, holiness, and righteousness are expressed, we see truthfulness, dignity, righteousness, purity, loveliness, and the quality of being well spoken of, all of which are virtues worthy of praise.

Due to Satan's temptation, man sinned and fell, thereby having the sinful nature within. Yet the good nature in man, which was created by God, still exists in man. For this reason, Confucian scholars spent a great deal of time to study whether the human nature is good or evil. Actually, the human nature originally created by God is good and virtuous. However, the sinful nature that came through the fall is evil. Therefore, today all descendants of Adam have both the good nature and the evil nature.

Our own experience can prove this point. After a person is born, he does not need to be taught to pursue goodness. He has a predisposition to strive upward and to do good. When he obeys and honors his parents, he feels at ease inside. If he provokes his parents to anger, lies to them, or disobeys them, he is convicted in his conscience. This proves that there is a good nature in man. In the same manner, after we are born, without being taught and without any learning, we automatically lie to our parents and cheat them, and evil words and thoughts well up in us. After we sin, lie, or do something filthy, on the one hand we feel regretful and sorrowful, but on the other hand we want to improve ourselves. This proves that we have the good nature as well as the evil nature.

THE IMAGE OF LOVE, LIGHT, HOLINESS, AND RIGHTEOUSNESS CORRESPONDING TO THE REALITY OF THE DIVINE LIFE

God created us in His image of love, light, holiness, and righteousness. After the fall He also ordained that the Lord Jesus would become a man and pass through death and resurrection to become the Spirit to enter into us who believe in Him to be our life and content. The intrinsic nature of this life fully corresponds to the image of God—love, light, holiness, and righteousness. Today the Lord Jesus, who became flesh, died, and resurrected, is the living Spirit, and as such, He enters into all those who believe into Him, just like air entering into us.

In the Bible God uses air to illustrate that the Lord is the breath of life to us (John 20:22). The breath of life cannot be seen or touched but is very real to our human life. If we do not breathe for five minutes, we will die. Just as our physical life needs air, the life in our spirit, which is higher than our physical life, is a matter of Jesus as the breath of life, the Spirit of life, coming into us to be our life. The constituents of Him as life are love, light, holiness, and righteousness. He is the embodiment of love, light, holiness, and righteousness.

We human beings were created with a predisposition toward love, light, holiness, and righteousness, yet we do not have the real elements of love, light, holiness, and righteousness. This may be likened to the fact that the photograph of a person has the person's outward form and posture but not his inward reality of life. Man has an inner desire to do good, but when he is actually going to do good, it is an entirely different story. Therefore, Romans 7:18b says, "For to will is present with me, but to work out the good is not." We have only the form of goodness. We have the shell of love, light, holiness, and righteousness, but not the intrinsic substance of love, light, holiness, and righteousness. When we receive the Lord Jesus as life, He as the embodiment of love, light, holiness, and righteousness enters into us to be our life elements. Therefore, God's way is not to improve our behavior outwardly. God's salvation is that Christ enters into us to be our life that we may have Him as life and live by Him. It is the Lord Jesus who brings us the reality of life.

ENJOYING THE SPIRIT OF LIFE
BY CALLING ON THE NAME OF THE LORD
AND THEREBY BEING FULL OF
THE MARVELOUS POWER OF LIFE

We all have the experience that before we were saved, even though we wanted to listen to our parents and honor them, we could not do so. Now whenever we call on the Lord Jesus, He enters into us so that we can spontaneously honor our parents and obey them. Many young people were previously not allowed by their parents to believe in Jesus. Now, however, because these young people have a real change in their life, the parents no longer oppose them after seeing in them the living testimony of believing in Jesus.

In addition, many times, no matter how parents try to discipline, restrain, admonish, or show their love to their children, it is hard for the children to change. Then one day the children hear the gospel, believe, receive the Lord Jesus, and call, "O Lord Jesus, I love You. I receive You as my Savior and my life." From that time, not only are they full of joy within, but they are also full of the power to do good.

Luke 19 records the story of the salvation of the sinner Zaccheus. He was a tax collector collecting taxes from the Jews for the Roman Empire. He often used the authority of the Roman Empire to extort money from his own fellow countrymen. One day Jesus Himself came to the city where he lived. Since he was small in stature and could not see Jesus in the crowd, he climbed up in a sycamore tree in order to see Him. Looking up, Jesus saw this lost one and said to him, "Zaccheus, hurry and come down, for today I must stay in your house" (v. 5). Zaccheus received Jesus on that day and had a revolutionary change. He said, "The half of my possessions, Lord, I give to the poor, and if I have taken anything from anyone by false accusation, I restore four times as much" (v. 8). Apparently, the Lord Jesus was standing outside of Zaccheus, but in reality He could be the dynamic salvation to him. In the same way today, if a person calls, "Lord," the Spirit of the Lord enters into him with an inconceivable power which causes him to have a radical change in his inner nature which is expressed in his outward action.

Therefore, the life of a Christian is not a life of correcting the outward conduct but a life of allowing Christ to enter in to be the motivating power. Take the example of a car. If instead of filling up the gas tank and charging the battery, someone tries to use his own strength to make a car run by pushing or pulling it, that will be a very difficult task. If we want a car to run, first we need to completely fill the gas tank and fully charge the battery. In this way the car will be able to run. Today, because people do not have a full understanding of God's salvation, in their lives they are like cars without gas and electricity. They depend either on others to pull them from ahead or on their relatives and friends to push them from behind. However, all the pushing results in no movement. Not only so, the car is overturned. This way is altogether wrong. We need the Lord Jesus just as a car needs gas and electricity. The Lord Jesus as the Spirit of life is the "gas and electricity." If we have the Lord Jesus, we are like cars filled up with gas and fully charged with electricity. By calling "O Lord Jesus," we can run.

Before a person believes in the Lord he is like a car without gas and electricity. After he believes in the Lord, there is no need for others to pull and drag him. Just by calling "O Lord Jesus," he can experience the bountiful supply of the Spirit of Jesus Christ. The drastic changes in the saved ones often cause their relatives, friends, and neighbors to be astonished. The marvelous thing is that if we call on other names such as Confucius, there is no response. However, once we call "O Lord Jesus," we have a feeling within. This is the living Spirit of the Lord Jesus in us. Even though we cannot fully comprehend what this is, once the Lord as the "fresh air" comes into us, our whole being is made comfortable and happy. This is truly our experience. Once we call "O Lord Jesus," we receive Him as the embodiment of love, light, holiness, and righteousness. Such a One matches our God-created image of love, light, holiness, and righteousness. As a result, what we are within exactly matches what we are without. In this way, what we do will be true, dignified, righteous, pure, lovely, and well spoken of.

EXPERIENCING THE SALVATION OF LIFE
BY CALLING ON THE NAME OF THE LORD

I have seen some young people who in their age of "metamorphosis" were haughty and arrogant, but by unceasingly calling "O Lord Jesus" day after day, they have become dignified and mature. Previously, they always liked to "put up their fists," but now there is Someone in them—the Lord

Jesus—who draws their fists back. We all have experiences like this. Sometimes we are about to lose our temper, and sometimes our temper has even reached the tip of our tongue, but the Lord Jesus gives us a pull, and we turn and go into our room to call, "O Lord Jesus! O Lord Jesus!" Then our temper is extinguished.

Everyone who believes in Jesus has a wonderful fountain, a "fire hydrant," within. Once we call "O Lord Jesus," the fire hydrant is turned on, and it flows out water to quench our anger. Previously when we went shopping, if the sales person gave us more change than we were owed, we would be happy that we had gained some advantage. But now instead of feeling excited about it, we return the extra change. The Lord Jesus has turned many naughty students into "saints." This is the operation of His salvation in them to make them people who are true, dignified, righteous, pure, lovely, and well spoken of, people who are full of virtues. This is not through outward teaching, nor is it through outward correction, but it is through the metabolism carried out in man by the Lord Jesus as his life. This is God's salvation.

Do not ever think that Christians are those who belong to a charitable organization with the purpose of doing good deeds. We are not drawing people to join a religion and then teaching them to change their outward behavior. The first lines of the chorus of *Hymns,* #538 read, "It is God's intent and pleasure / That His Christ be wrought in me." When a person receives God's salvation by believing in the Lord Jesus, he does not receive some teaching outwardly for the correction of his behavior. Rather, he receives the living Christ into him to be his life.

I hope that each brother and sister who has been saved can clearly see this matter. Do not ever exercise your will to do good, for doing so often has the opposite effect. God does not require us to exercise our will to do good. Instead, He wants us to call on the name of Jesus. The Bible says, "Whoever calls on the name of the Lord shall be saved" (Rom. 10:13). When we were giving messages in America on calling on the name of the Lord, some people thought that we were teaching another philosophy, and some considered calling on the Lord a kind of mental exercise. Instead of debating with them, we simply asked them to call on other names such as Washington and Socrates to see if they would sense anything different. Those who tried it did not get any feeling. We have to know that calling "Lord Jesus" is a tremendous matter.

When we call, He comes into us. As the resurrected One, He comes into us with God's life to save us. If you feel unhappy or uncomfortable, you can open to Him individually, calling, "O Lord Jesus." If you call this way several times, you will feel at ease within. The Lord Jesus is our Savior, who saves us not only from perdition but also from our temper, anger, lies, and jealousy. He is our way of salvation, and He is our salvation.

CONCLUSION

First, God created us according to His image of love, light, holiness, and righteousness so that we have the predisposition toward what is true, dignified, righteous, pure, lovely, and well spoken of. Yet all these are just outward forms and frames; there is no reality within. Therefore, in His salvation God caused Christ to become the Spirit so that Christ as the embodiment of love, light, holiness, and righteousness can enter into us. This One who comes into us corresponds with our image which was originally created by God. Therefore, once He enters into us, He fills the outer shell created by God so that we can be full of reality. This is the same as a glove. Although the glove is designed according to the image of the hand, it is floppy and empty without the hand. But when the glove contains the hand, it has reality. Only then can it fully express the image of the hand, and the hand can also move freely.

The Lord Jesus in whom we believe is the One who is love, light, holiness, and righteousness. Through us He is expressed as our virtues: as truthfulness, dignity, righteousness, purity, loveliness, and the quality of being well spoken of. Consequently, the intrinsic nature of the living we manifest before man is virtue, yet for others it becomes something worthy of praise. Once the Lord Jesus enters into man, He makes the God-created man full of the inward reality that he may express the God who is love, light, holiness, and righteousness and become true, dignified, righteous, pure, lovely, and well spoken of. Once the Lord enters into us, all our problems spontaneously are solved. Once He enters into us, all our inward needs are fully supplied. Thus, we are those who have obtained Christ, who live Christ, and who express Christ.

(A message given on April 19, 1987 at the Lord's table meeting in Taipei.)

THE GOSPEL WE ANNOUNCE

Scripture Reading: Gal. 2:20

It is a very joyful thing that there are so many newly saved brothers and sisters who came from various villages and towns to break bread with us. Though we cannot shake hands and greet each one of you, we believe we do love one another in the one Lord. He is our Lord, and He is also the Lord of the brothers and sisters from these villages and towns. We all have one Lord and one life, we enjoy one salvation, and we are in one Body.

Because of the sovereign grace of the Lord, in these few years through the Full-time Training in Taipei the Lord has prepared almost two hundred brothers and sisters who have gone to the villages and towns to announce the gospel and set up churches. We do worship Him for this. For over a year now we have seen the fruitful result. At the time when the outreach to the villages was about to set off, I could not go myself since I was in America. I made long distance calls to the ones going out and talked to them over the phone. Now, seeing such a result, I truly rejoice.

CHRIST DYING FOR OUR SINS
ACCORDING TO THE SCRIPTURES

The gospel which we announce is "Christ died for our sins according to the Scriptures," as declared in 1 Corinthians 15:3. The first crucial point of the gospel is that because of His love for us, our dear Savior became flesh, passed through human living, and finally on the cross gave up His body, shedding His precious blood to accomplish an eternal redemption. We were all sinners, yet the Lord loved us and died for our sins that we may be redeemed. Moreover, He was buried and was "raised on the third day according to the Scriptures" (v. 4). This portion of the Word in 1 Corinthians 15 mentions "according to the Scriptures" twice, the first time in conjunction with His dying for our sins and the second time with His being raised on the third day. This is truly glad tidings—the dead can be raised. What a miracle that the Lord Jesus was raised from the dead!

This principle of death and resurrection can be seen everywhere in the universe. For example, any kind of seed after having been sown into the ground dies first and then bears much fruit. If there is no death, there is no life. Because the seed which falls into the ground has this kind of life, it is not terminated by death. On the contrary, through death it grows and bears much fruit. After the Lord Jesus died and was buried, those who hated Him and plotted to kill Him had a great celebration. However, they did not know that in a matter of less than three days, this Jesus who had died was raised. His death was a death with accomplishments, and His resurrection was a resurrection with even greater accomplishments. The chorus of *Hymns*, #227 says, "Thine the cup of suff'ring, / Mine the cup of blessing; / For Thy love in Thy redemption, / Praise we ever sing!" Through the death of the Lord Jesus our sins were dealt with, and through His resurrection we have received His life.

DYING FOR *OUR SINS*

Through His death the Lord accomplished many things for us. First, He died for the sins of each one of us (1 Cor. 15:3; 1 Pet. 2:24; Gal. 1:4; Heb. 9:28). As believers of the Lord, we all confess that we are sinful. Even though it has been over sixty years since I have received the Lord, I still have to confess that I am sinful. Every morning when I pray to the Lord, I still have to confess my sins, such as losing my temper and speaking too rashly. Even though such things are not big sins, all trespasses, whether big or small, are sins before God.

Every morning when we draw near to the Lord, we have to "wash our hands" and confess. Confessing is like the washing of hands. We have to wash our hands many times a day because we touch many filthy things every day. In the same manner, in our experience we may not speak anything sinful, yet we often commit sins in our thoughts. Whenever we think of others, it is always easy for us to think of their wrongdoings. When we think of our parents, we ought to remember their love in raising us. Yet instead, what we often remember is how they do not understand us and how they have mistreated us. Once we think of our children, we think of how they do not appreciate us and how they do not obey us. Whenever we consider, we commit sins. Moreover, whenever we open our mouth, we commit transgressions. This is why the Chinese have a saying: "Calamities come from the mouth." Yet it is impossible for us not to think and not to speak. Therefore, after one day our entire being has been contaminated. At this time, we need to draw near to the Lord and confess our sins to Him. He is the One who is holy and sinless. As long as we confess to Him, He forgives us and cleanses us of all our sins.

If we say that after we have received the Lord we do not sin, that is a lie (1 John 1:8). After we receive the Lord, we should not sin, but we may still sin. Even Paul said, "But the evil which I do not will, this I practice" (Rom. 7:19). This proves that after we are saved, we may still be overcome by sin occasionally. Yet after we have sinned, as promised in 1 John 1, as long as we confess to God, He forgives us, and the blood of Jesus cleanses us from every sin (vv. 7-9). Every day we need to apply the blood of the Lord Jesus for the cleansing of our sins. In this way we can maintain the fellowship we have with God.

DYING FOR *US*

The Lord Jesus not only died for *our sins,* but even more He died for *us* (2 Cor. 5:14-15). We were worthy of death and perdition, but He died for us. This is a glad tiding. In His dying for us the Lord Jesus bore not only our sins but also our whole being. We all were included in His death. This may be compared to what happened two to three hundred years ago when the ancestors of the Taiwanese migrated from Fukien to Taiwan. All the Taiwanese were included in that migration and crossed the sea to Taiwan. This is because they are joined to their ancestors and are included in them.

Likewise, we all died in the death of the Lord Jesus. The Lord Jesus died, and we also died, because all those who believe in the Lord are joined to Him as one (1 Cor. 6:17). The first stanza of *Hymns,* #233 says, "O what a miracle, my Lord, / That I'm in Thee and Thou in me, / That Thou and I are really one; / O what a wondrous mystery!" We have nothing good to give to the Lord, yet we can partake of all the good things in Him. When He was crucified, we were crucified with Him because we were in Him.

RESURRECTED FOR US AND LIVING IN US

The Lord Jesus is God who became flesh with a physical form, a body, with flesh and bones, and as such, He died for our sins on the cross and was buried. Then after three days He was resurrected and transfigured into the Spirit, the life-giving Spirit, to enter into us as life. Therefore, not only did He die for us, but He also resurrected for us. We who believe in the Lord Jesus not only receive the forgiveness of sins, but we also have Him in us as life.

Before we believe in the Lord, we have nothing to do with the Lord Jesus. However, after we receive Him as our Savior, He begins to bother us from within. He does not want to do the things we want to do, and we do not want to do the things He wants to do. The two, He and we, are in discord. Sometimes, we are in harmony with the Lord, and we pray in our morning prayer, "Lord Jesus, I love You. I want to obey You." Nevertheless, in the afternoon when we come across something that we like but He does not like, He troubles us within so that we have no peace for the whole afternoon. This is so in particular for the sisters, who in the past, when they went shopping in department stores, simply bought whatever they pleased. However, when they go shopping after they have believed in Jesus, the moment they pick up a dress, within them Jesus may say, "Put it down and go home." If they would not obey and put it down, thinking that they may be missing an opportunity unless they buy it, the Lord will say, "Do not reason! Put it down and go home." Eventually though, they may still buy it, but they will not have peace within. We all have this kind of experience. It is so good to have the Lord Jesus in us giving us peace and joy all the time. However, because He is holy, when we do something that is incompatible with His nature, He troubles us within and makes us restless.

In our daily life the Lord Jesus always does this kind of thing. Sometimes when we grumble to our mother, the Lord Jesus bothers us within, so we have no other way but to obey. Finally, we can only confess to Him and say, "Lord, I am really corrupt. I have broken my mother's heart again." Nevertheless, sometimes we truly cannot obey, and we immediately lose our temper with our mother. After the incident, however, we regret and come to the Lord, confessing to Him, "O Lord, I am really bad. Please forgive me of my sins." We all have this kind of experience. We surely can sympathize with one another because we all have the same problem. The Lord Jesus often bothers us in this manner, proving that He truly lives inside us. This is His grace to us.

When the Lord Jesus was crucified, we were crucified with Him. When He was resurrected, we were also resurrected with Him. Furthermore, now He lives in us. Whenever we live in Christ, that is the time we have joy. Even though we had our first birth through our parents, our spirit was deadened because of our sins (Eph. 2:1). However, we were regenerated through the resurrection of the Lord Jesus (v. 5). Before we believed in the Lord, we were active outwardly but dead in our spirit. However, after we have believed in the Lord Jesus, when we exercise our spirit by calling on His name, our spirit within is enlivened. The resurrected Jesus as the life-giving Spirit not only regenerated us, but also lives in us and makes us His home (v. 22).

Ephesians 3:17 says that Christ wants to make His home in our hearts. Once He makes His home in our hearts and lives in us, we have Him as our Lord. Before we were saved, we were pitiful because we were wandering about and were lost. After we are saved, because He is living in us, we have Him as our Lord, and we are blessed because we are under His preserving and cherishing. Regardless of whether people believe in Confucius, Buddha, or the sea goddess Matsu, they cannot and dare not say that the one in whom they believe is the Lord. Only those who believe in Jesus say they believe in the Lord, because only Jesus is Lord.

JOINED TO THE LORD AS ONE SPIRIT

Paul said, "I am crucified with Christ; and it is no longer I who live, but it is Christ who lives in me" (Gal. 2:20). As God, the Lord Jesus left His throne in heaven and came to the earth to be a man in the flesh. Then He was crucified on the cross, He died, He was buried, and He resurrected. In His death in which He bore our sins, He not only dealt with our sins, but by bringing us with Him in His crucifixion, He also dealt with us, the sinners. Furthermore, through His death and resurrection, He was transfigured to be the Spirit and came into us to regenerate us that we may live with Him and be one with Him.

He died for our redemption, and He was raised for our justification. Now He is living in us as the living Savior. This is the gospel which we announce. The Lord Jesus has come into us. We and He, He and we, are joined as one. First Corinthians 6:17 says, "He who is joined to the Lord is one spirit." He as the Spirit has become one with our spirit; the two spirits have become one spirit. In His salvation the Lord is able to save us to such an extent. What a gospel this is!

(A message given on April 16, 1990 at the Lord's table meeting in Taipei.)

Chapter Six

OUR CHURCH LIFE

(1)

AN EXCELLENT LOCATION
FOR THE PRACTICE OF THE NEW WAY

Taiwan is truly a good location that is most suitable for us to start practicing the new way, because the life here is stable and secure, education is at a high level and available to all, the economic condition and public security are extremely good, and transportation is especially convenient. In particular, we should be grateful for the various conveniences provided by the government which facilitate the gospel. This is a rare opportunity and a rare location.

In 1984 we compiled official statistics, which included more than six hundred churches from the six major continents over the whole earth. Today in less than three years, the total number of churches on the whole earth has increased from over six hundred localities to more than eight hundred localities. In addition, the number of churches is evenly split between the East and the West, which is very marvelous. More than four hundred churches are in the Far East and Australia, and more than four hundred churches are in the Western Hemisphere. These eight hundred or more churches are spread out in more than forty countries on the six major continents.

Currently, the country with the greatest number of churches is the United States, with a total of more than one hundred. Why then do we choose Taiwan as the place to begin to practice the new way? It is because the population here is concentrated and because we have had forty years of history here since we first arrived in 1949. We believe the various conditions here are very suitable for us. Of course, many brothers and sisters have come from overseas to join the training and to coordinate with the move of the Body. Therefore, due to the different needs, the expense is relatively high, yet we feel that no matter how we look at it, this is the best place for us to start practicing the new way.

THE MEANING AND BASIS OF THE WORD *CHURCH*

The Lord has already added to us many newly saved brothers and sisters, and we also have had meetings with the new ones in their homes. However, we truly desire to have an opportunity at this time to come together so that we can know each other better. Since many new believers have just entered into the church life, we would like to clarify where we stand among the many sects of Christianity. Some have heard that we are called "the church in Taipei," so they ask, "Which church in Taipei? What kind of name is this? Why do you use a general term as the name of your group?" I believe many of you desire to know more concerning this matter. Here we would like to briefly explain this practice and the reason behind it.

The title of this message is "Our Church (*Chao-hui*) Life." The title is simple, but the implication is quite extensive. Generally, people are familiar with the term *chiao-hui* (religious society), but our usage of *chao-hui* (assembly) in place of *chiao-hui* does have a basis. In the Bible the Greek word for *church* is *ekklesia,* which is composed of two words, *ek* and *klesia. Ek* means "out," and *klesia* means "called"; the composition of these two words means "the called-out ones." Thus, the Greek word refers to all the called-out ones within a city. In the New Testament times this is the word the Lord Jesus used when He mentioned the church in speaking to the disciples. This word includes the meaning of a "hui" (society or congregation) but not the meaning of "chiao" (religion). It also includes the meaning of "chao" (call).

From 1860 to 1870, after some brothers in the United States were raised up, they studied the English word *church.* The origin of this word can be traced back to a Germanic word

which is mainly used to refer to the building where Christians
gather for church services. During the nineteenth century,
the Brethren of England felt this word could not express the
significance of *ekklesia* in the Bible, so they changed *church*
to *assembly* in their hymnals, in their Bibles, and in all their
literature. *Assembly* means "the called-out congregation."
Therefore, we are not the first ones to use the word *chao-hui*
(assembly). After 1915, a charismatic movement began in the
United States which established a group, the Assemblies of
God. Seventy years ago it spread to China, and in Chinese
their name was translated as *shen-chao-hui* (God's assembly
or God-called congregation). Thus, this word was very appro-
priately translated by a group of brothers according to the
original meaning in the Bible.

Recently we have begun to work on publishing the Chinese
Recovery Version of the New Testament. This translation is
being produced according to the Greek text, using the current
Chinese Union Version as a reference, with modifications and
annotations. During this process, we felt that since we are
making a new translation, we should change the incorrect
translation of *chiao-hui* (religious society) to that of *chao-hui*
(assembly). Therefore, from now on we will use *chao-hui*
instead of *chiao-hui* in all of our publications in order to
convey the proper meaning.

When the Western missionaries first came to China and
were translating the word *ekklesia,* they said that according
to the word *tzung-chiao* (religion), this "hui" (society or
congregation) is a kind of "chiao-hui" (religious society); thus,
the word *chiao-hui* came into existence. Of course, back then
there was no such word in the Chinese vocabulary. This term
chiao-hui was invented by the members of the Imperial
Academy and the elderly Chinese scholars who were hired
by the Western missionaries who came over to China to
preach the gospel and translate the Bible. Today many other
religions also use this word, such as *fo-chiao-hui* (Buddhist
religious society). Therefore, we feel that it really needs to be
changed. Today the Buddhists call themselves *fo-chiao-hui,*
but they would not call themselves *fo-chao-hui* (Buddha-called
congregation). Only the church of the Lord is a called-out

congregation, so it only makes sense that it should be called *chao-hui* (assembly). However, due to the conventions established in society, to outsiders we still refer to ourselves as *chiao-hui* (religious society), but actually we take *chao-hui* (assembly) as the proper expression.

THE ORIGIN OF THE CHURCH LIFE

Our church life began in 1920. At that time the Lord raised up in China a group of young people, mostly college students. Later in Foochow the Lord gained a young student by the name of Watchman Nee. Since his grandfather had been a pastor, he was a third-generation Christian. However, he was not assured of his salvation until he was seventeen years old, in the year 1920. Shortly after he was saved, he fervently loved the Bible. He was very good at studying; he not only knew the Bible well, but he also saw much light in the Scriptures. He compared the truth and revelations in the Bible with the various conditions in Christianity at the time and discovered that many things in Christianity are not found in the Bible.

At that time Brother Nee was a sophomore in college, and he was very proficient in the English language. Therefore, he read many books published in English and also many biographies and lectures of famous people, and he also thoroughly studied the history of Christianity. He deeply felt the need to put something into practice—a group of Christians in China coming together to meet and to worship according to the Bible. That was the beginning of the meeting among us.

In this way, the first meeting took place in 1922 in Foochow. In 1949 the brothers felt that a portion of the saints should leave mainland China and go overseas for the spread of the Lord's work. So that year a group of brothers and I came to Taiwan. Back then the number of saints who came from the mainland was at most four or five hundred. These four or five hundred saints spread throughout the major cities in Taiwan and began to meet. Soon afterward I was invited to the Philippines. I worked in this way for ten years, going back and forth. In 1961 I deeply felt that we should start the work in the West, so I went to the United States to observe the situation there. In the following year, 1962, I received the burden, settled down in the United States, and began this recovery work in English, which has continued to this day.

CRUCIAL MATTERS IN THE CHURCH LIFE
ON THE NEGATIVE SIDE

Eliminating Denominational Divisions

We are speaking of the church life in particular for a few reasons. First, we hope to eliminate denominational divisions. The situation of denominational divisions is the outward, present condition of Christianity. Of course, this divisive condition of denominations has not come into existence only recently. This situation of denominational division began, at the latest, from the time of Luther during the Reformation and has continued to this day. Certainly this is not according to the Bible at all. However, this kind of situation had occurred at an even earlier time, in the time of the apostles. For example, some among the believers in the church in Corinth went as far as saying that they were of Paul, others said that they were of Cephas, and still others said that they were of Apollos; one faction who thought highly of themselves told others that they were of Christ (1 Cor. 1:12). Paul very much detested this and exhorted them to do away with this situation.

Therefore, since we worship God according to the Bible, we cannot accept the traditional denominations nor participate in the traditional divisions. Therefore, we do not take a particular name; we say only that we are Christians. We truly do not desire to take another name. This may be compared to the natural world in which there is only one moon. In the United States there is the one moon, in all the countries in Asia there is the one moon, and in Europe there is still just the one moon. The moon is simply the moon. If you must give it a name, calling it "the moon in the United States," or "the moon in Taiwan," it is all right. But regardless of what you call it, it is still the same moon; it simply appears in various places. For this reason, we are very careful with the matter of name.

However, in this age and in any country, as long as there is a religious gathering or a religious activity, it must be officially registered with the government for permission. That is why we applied and registered with the government as "Assembly Hall of the Church in Taipei." Normally, we still call ourselves the church in a certain place. For example, in Hong Kong we are "the church in Hong Kong," in Taipei we are "the church in Taipei," and in New York we are "the church in New York," and so forth.

We do not recognize denominations because we do not agree with division. All believers, regardless of their differences in the doctrine or practice of baptism, as long as they have genuinely believed in the Lord and received the Lord, are those who belong to the Lord as the members of the church. If they are in Taipei, they are the members of the church in Taipei; if they go to Los Angeles, they are in the church in Los Angeles. This principle saves us from the division of denominations.

Abolishing the Clergy System

Second, the clergy system must be abolished from our church life. The so-called "clergy system" is a group of people in Christianity who, after studying theology and receiving a theological education, come out to do the evangelical and ministerial work. In a typical Christian organization, we can see a group of people who are the preachers, pastors, teachers, and choir directors. They are the clergy. Once these clergymen come to a meeting, all the other saints merely sit there passively. Related to the church, the saints do not have to do anything other than attend the meeting and offer money, because from the time they are saved, they are never taught to do anything.

According to the Bible this practice is altogether against God's desire. God desires all who are saved to be the members of the Body of Christ. The church is the Body of Christ, just as we have our physical body. This body has different members, and different members have different functions. If all the members of my body do not function accordingly, I will become paralyzed and numb; my body will not be a body anymore.

This is the general condition of Christianity today. Only the clergy is active in the meetings, and the congregation is inactive. Metaphorically speaking, the saints are not living; they have become numb. According to the Bible we can never accept this. Therefore, among us we do not want the so-called preachers and pastors and other practices of the clergy system. We hope that some brothers and sisters will be able to serve the Lord full-time, but this does not mean that being full-time is their lifelong occupation. If this year they come out to serve the Lord full-time, and after four years they have the leading from the Lord and are willing to do something else, then they can go and do according to the Lord's leading. This is like the apostle Paul; although he was the greatest gospel preacher, he did not have preaching the gospel as his job. On the one hand, Paul preached the gospel, but on the other hand, he made tents with his own hands. He did not make tents for his own living only; he even labored with his hands to provide for the needs of those who served and preached the gospel with him (Acts 18:3; 20:34).

According to the Bible, therefore, there is not a profession of "preacher." We are now encouraging the saved college students not to go to work immediately after graduation but to spend one or two years learning to serve full-time, if possible. On the one hand, they will endeavor in the learning of truth, getting to know the spiritual things, and on the other hand, they will be exercised in the matter of service in the house of God. If after two years, after they have been equipped in this way, they go out to get a job or do some business, this will be very good. Therefore, we truly hope that every brother and sister can be perfected and participate in some kind of service. Some brothers and sisters may feel that they can go full-time right away; that would be the best. Some may feel that they can go half-time and some one-quarter time, while some may feel that they can set apart their nights and holidays. These all serve the Lord; these are all good. In any case, we all should minister; we should all participate in some kind of service.

At this time there is a meeting in almost every home, and we very much encourage all who are saved in each household—the husband, the wife, the children, and the parents, every member of the household—to be active in the home meetings. For example, the little brother can call a hymn, the big sister can pray, the older brother can read the Bible, and the younger brother can say a little word. Everyone can function in a home meeting, building up one another. Of course, the new believers may not know very much, so some who have been saved for a longer time need to have a home meeting with them. This is not going to their homes to be their family pastor or their family preacher; it is to meet together with them as a saint in the church.

We do not have preachers, we do not have pastors, and we do not have gospel giants preaching the gospel while others listen. We are simply a group of saints—some only eighteen, nineteen, or twenty years old accompanied by one or two older ones—going out together to knock on doors and visit people to bring the gospel to them. Thank the Lord, people are happy and willing to open the door and receive us. This is truly the work of the grace of the Lord. Therefore, we all need to see that there is no clergy system in our church life.

Tearing Down Religious Hierarchy

Third, we need to tear down religious hierarchy. The clergy system turns the saints into "laymen." In Christianity there are two groups of people attending worship services: one group is the clergy, and the other group is the common believers other than the clergy, the "laymen," who merely attend worship services and listen to the clergy's preaching. In our church life, however, there are only the brothers and sisters, only the members of the Body of Christ, each carrying out his function. There is no clergy system.

The clergy system is related to religious hierarchy, so in order to abolish the clergy system, religious hierarchy must be torn down. This may not sound like a good idea at first. An ordinary person might say, "Religion is good because it teaches people to do good. If religious hierarchy were torn down, would the world not be in chaos?" Here what we call hierarchy is *hierarchia* in Greek, which is a group of clergymen from among Christians organized into a system of religious hierarchy. For example, the pope has the highest rank in Catholicism; this is a kind of religious hierarchy.

Some time ago when I was touring the Vatican, there were only seventy or eighty cardinals, commonly called "red-robed bishops," serving at the side of the pope as his cabinet. Now there are more than one hundred. They are referred to in this way because they all wear red robes. Under the "red-robed bishops" are the other bishops, and under these bishops are still various ranks, all the way down to the monks and nuns. This is the organized system composed of their clergy, which is a religious system. Besides Catholicism, Protestantism also has denomination after denomination, each with its clerical hierarchy. For instance, the Episcopal Church has bishops, the Presbyterian Church has pastors and a presbytery, and the Baptist Church has not a presbytery but a system of pastors. These are all religious hierarchies.

The Old Practice Killing
the Organic Function of the Saints

We must destroy and tear down these three things—denominational divisions, the clergy system, and religious hierarchy—because they kill the functions of the saints as the members of the Body. These denominations, systems, and hierarchies depend on domination, and domination is a kind of bondage. This is the reason why Christianity today has deteriorated, degraded, and even become corrupted. Indeed, we see that when the clergy system becomes an organization, it controls, dominates, and puts the saints under bondage, causing them to lose the functions they should have as the members of the Body of Christ.

After years of study and seeking before the Lord, in 1985 we felt that we should thoroughly correct our situation. This is because in all these years, although we have rejected denominations, the clergy system, and religious hierarchy, the way we meet and the way we preach the gospel have fallen mostly into forms; they are too rigid. This is indeed unavoidable, for the church has been on the earth for nearly two thousand years, and the traditional way of meeting after so many years has evolved into the situation of one person speaking and everyone else listening. Christians gather together and hire an eloquent person to speak to the congregation; this is the traditional way of meeting. As for gospel preaching, it is also a matter of finding a large place of gathering and inviting people to come to listen to the gospel. These traditional practices are not evident in the Bible; therefore, their efficiency is very low.

Because of the need for research, I did my best to investigate the statistics of the increase in the number of people in Christianity. After I investigated for a few years, up to the end of October of 1986, the report I received was that four out of the five major denominations had not increased in number, but instead, the number decreased greatly. Consider the example of Taiwan. Currently the population of Taiwan is at least nineteen million, but out of these nineteen million there are less than five hundred thousand Christians. There are more than three million six hundred thousand Buddhists and more than one million Taoists, yet the number of Christians barely reaches five hundred thousand. This means that for every one hundred Taiwan residents, there are only two and a half Christians.

Christianity was first brought to Taiwan by the Presbyterian Church of Scotland. It has been more than one hundred fifty years since then, but today their number is only somewhere between ten and twenty thousand. Statistically, we have over forty thousand people, second only to the Presbyterian Church. In any case, these numbers all reveal that less than three out of one hundred people in Taiwan are Christians. How pitiful this condition is!

The reason behind all this is none other than the traditional practice in Christianity, which not only kills the functions of Christians but also numbs the Christians themselves. This practice renders all the saints "unemployed," unable to do anything. Christianity has had to take the way of seminaries and of recruiting theology students in order to train a group of clergymen who specialize in doing ministerial work. When these clergymen want to do something, they gather a congregation to maintain their clerical position. This gathering kills and nullifies people's functions and numbs the people. That is why we can say that this practice has no power whatsoever.

In 1962 I settled down in the United Stated and started to work. In 1964 I began to compile statistics. That year I obtained some numbers: The whole United States had a population of over two hundred million, half of which, one hundred million, were Christians. Among them, fifty-five percent were Protestants, and forty-five percent were Catholics. In other words, there were fifty to sixty million people in Protestantism in 1964. These fifty to sixty million people, after twenty-two years of work, increased by a total of nine million. By simply looking at the number *nine million* you may feel it is big, but if you look carefully, the base number was fifty to sixty million. This means that there was less than one percent increase per year. Perhaps among one hundred people, not one person had led someone to believe in the Lord in a whole year. Only about 0.5 percent of the people were led to believe in the Lord. This power is really very small.

In the last ten years we also have lost the power of increase here. For this reason we are stirred up and forced to take the new way. At this time, after more than two years of research, not only have we changed the way, but we also have put it into practice. In the Full-time Training, five to six hundred people are carrying out the experiment every day, and after three and a half months of testing, we have seen that it is a definite success. If we walk according to the new way, in one year the total number of people will increase at least threefold, and the number of functioning and useful ones will at least double. I hope that everyone will see this clearly. In conclusion, we are emphasizing putting aside the negative things. We reject denominational divisions, we abolish the clergy system, and we completely tear down religious hierarchy.

THINGS TO PRACTICE IN THE CHURCH LIFE ON THE POSITIVE SIDE

Preaching a Pure, High, and Complete Gospel

Today there are two main things that we have to do on the

positive side. First, we have to proclaim a pure, high, and complete gospel. "Pure" means without mixture. Today the gospel preached in Christianity is mixed and impure. This reminds us of the parable the Lord Jesus spoke to us in Matthew 13, about a woman taking leaven and hiding it in the meal (v. 33). We know that the meal is Christ Himself, but today's Christianity takes leaven and mixes it with teachings concerning Christ, thus confusing the pure truth of Christ.

Furthermore, the gospel preached in Christianity today is too shallow. They preach merely things like the forgiveness of sins and deliverance from hell. These are certainly correct, but they are too shallow. We all know that the growth of any creature requires an outer skin and also an inner content. For example, in order for a baby chicken to grow up, it must have feathers and skin on the outside so that muscle can grow on the inside. Today the gospel preached in Christianity is a "skin-and-feathers gospel," which speaks only about the brevity and sorrow of human life and how believing in Jesus results in not going to hell, having a better living, and receiving blessings and peace in the human life. These are all too shallow and cannot make known God's eternal economy, His eternal plan.

In preaching the gospel, the first thing we speak about is the mystery of human life and the meaning of human life. What is the meaning of human life? It is to be a vessel of God to contain God within us. We need to be persons who contain God, who are filled with God, and who take God as life, that we may become God's expression and God's declaration. This is full of light. This is a part of the pure and high gospel.

God Desiring All Men to Be Saved and to Come to the Full Knowledge of the Truth

Second, we need to lead people to come to the full knowledge of the truth. There are many books among us that have messages concerning the truth. When a new one is saved, we should set up a meeting in his home, of which our main purpose is to lead him to come to the knowledge of the truth. First Timothy 2:4 says, "Who desires all men to be saved and to come to the full knowledge of the truth." God desires all men to be saved and completely enter into the ministry of the truth. In short, God desires all men to be saved and also desires each of them to understand the truth.

We are here not criticizing but using facts as an illustration. Today we do not hear much truth in Christianity. The saddest thing is that in the chapels in the United States we hear of nothing but marriage, careers, or other things such as raising children, none of which is the pure and deep truth. The Lord has shown us and entrusted to us that we should speak the pure and deep truth. In Matthew 28, when the Lord Jesus had passed through death and resurrection, He came back in resurrection into the midst of the disciples and said to them, "All authority has been given to Me in heaven and on earth" (v. 18). In heaven or on earth, all authority has been given to Him; He is the Lord of heaven and earth. Therefore, He sent out the disciples with this authority and said to them, "Go therefore and disciple all the nations, baptizing them into the name of the Father and of the Son and of the Holy Spirit" (v. 19). This is to baptize them into the Triune God.

The Lord Jesus also said, "Teaching them to observe all that I have commanded you. And behold, I am with you all the days until the consummation of the age" (v. 20). On the surface, Christianity keeps this word, but if you go deeper, you will discover otherwise. I was born into a Christian family. I was a fourth-generation Christian according to my mother's side of the family. From childhood I never attended a school run by the Chinese; I always attended schools run by the Americans. I attended worship services from my youth, and the schools also forced us to attend them. I am quite clear about the whole condition of Christianity. The gospel and the truth they preach are very simple. Some of the Lord Jesus' words spoken in the Gospel of Matthew, for example, are not simple, but Christianity applies them in a simple way. For instance, in the Gospels the Lord said, "Come to Me all who toil and are burdened, and I will give you rest" (Matt. 11:28). He also said that we should love one another (John 15:12) and that we should be humble, so that whoever wants to become great among us shall be our servant and slave (Matt. 20:26-27). Christianity does not apply words such as these in a proper way.

John 14 through 16 speaks of the mystery of the Triune God—how the Triune God is the Father, the Son, and the Spirit, how the Son is in the Father and the Father is in the Son, and how the two are one. Furthermore, the Father and the Son, who are two yet one, are realized by the Spirit. This realizing Spirit has entered into us to abide with us, revealing to us all the reality of the Triune God within us—from the Father to the Son to the Spirit—that this reality may become our experience. Since my youth, I have never heard this kind of deep message in Christianity. However, in Matthew the Lord Jesus said that we should observe all that He has commanded us. The Lord also said, "Abide in Me and I in you" (John 15:4). The Lord was telling us that He, the Lord, lives inside of us through the Spirit as His reality. Therefore, the Spirit's coming and being inside of us is the Lord's being inside of us. Now the Father and the Son with the Spirit come together to us to make an abode with us. This means that the entire Triune God comes into us to abide with us (John 14:23). This is a deep truth in the Bible.

In addition, Matthew 5, 6, and 7 speak of the decree of the kingdom's constitution, which is also extremely profound, crucial, and practical. However, these truths have become veiled mysteries among today's Christians. No one understands them, and no one speaks about them.

Preaching according to the Bible Being Our Going to People

In the last days of this age, the Lord has raised us up and given us a twofold commission: on the one hand, we are to dispose of everything negative, and on the other hand, we are to preach to people—not in part but in full—the pure, high, and complete gospel. This preaching is not done through inviting a spiritual giant to do the speaking; that is not according to the Bible. The Lord wants us to go. We all know that the first time God came to man with the gospel was in Genesis 3. When man fell, he hid himself out of the fear of God. At that time, God did not call to him from the heavens, but He Himself came to the garden of Eden and called toward the place where Adam and Eve were hiding, saying, "Where are you?" (Gen. 3:8-9). God was the first to go to someone's "door" to pay him a visit. Four thousand years later God Himself became flesh, put on a physical body, and came among men as a man to go to men's doors to pay them a visit. He went to the door of Zaccheus, and He went into the house of Zaccheus (Luke 19:1-10). He also paid a visit to the Samaritan woman beside the well (John 4:1-42). During His three and a half years of preaching, He did much work of visiting, never doing anything by calling people to organize a meeting or inviting people to a meeting. For many years the precious truth among us has not been able to be spread because our practice is contrary to the principle in the Bible. Therefore, we need to go against our former practice, no longer inviting people to come but going to where people are.

Thirty years ago in Taiwan we saw a group of medical people who went out to give injections. They all rode bicycles, and on the bicycles was the sign, "Injections in Your Home." Not long ago in the United States the business of "food delivery" began, which specializes in delivering food to people's homes. Today our preaching of the gospel and the truth is not inviting people to our "restaurant" but delivering food to their homes. Not only do we need to know people's situation, but more importantly we need to preach to them the pure, high, and complete gospel. Then little by little we can teach them the pure, high, and complete truth. In this way the Lord will be able to gain a proper church prepared as His bride so that He can come back to marry us. This is our commission today.

(A message given in a conference on February 1, 1987 in Taipei.)

CHAPTER SEVEN

OUR CHURCH LIFE

(2)

Scripture Reading: Luke 10:1-6, 16; Matt. 28:19; John 15:4-5, 16

Today we have been called out of Christianity by the Lord to bear a testimony that is according to the Bible. The Bible shows us that the church on the earth is one universally, and it is absolutely in oneness. Therefore, we reject denominational divisions, we reject the clergy system, and we reject religious hierarchy. While we do have the elders' administration of the church among us, in this administration there is no rule or control. On the positive side, our first step is preaching a pure, high, and complete gospel. The second step is speaking and teaching the pure, high, and complete truth.

VISITING PEOPLE HOUSE BY HOUSE, LEADING THEM TO BELIEVE IN THE LORD AND BE BAPTIZED

What we mentioned above is a summary explanation of the principle. The specific practice includes the following points. First, we need to visit people house by house, that is, knocking on doors house by house to visit unbelievers and leading them to believe in the Lord and be baptized. This is clearly explained in Luke 10:1-6 and 16, Matthew 28:19, and John 15:4-5 and 16. The Gospel of Luke tells how the Lord Jesus Himself, when He was on the earth, sought out people place by place, just as He told Zaccheus, "For the Son of Man has come to seek and to save that which is lost" (19:10).

After the Lord Jesus came from the heavens to the earth, He did not come out to minister right away, because He had to

wait until He was full-grown. He stayed in Nazareth until He
was thirty years old. This is according to the Old Testament,
in which a man had to wait until he was thirty years old
before he could come out to minister as a priest. The Chinese
ancients also said that a man must be "thirty years of age to
stand on his own feet." The Lord Jesus waited until He was
thirty before coming out to do the work of preaching the word.
The way He preached was not like what is done in Christianity
today. Today even we have been influenced by Christianity,
preaching the gospel according to that unscriptural way. This
way is the way of setting up a meeting hall or a gospel chapel
and gathering together a congregation to listen to one person
preaching the gospel. We see in the Bible that the Lord Jesus
did not preach the gospel in such a way. The pattern in the
Bible which the Lord left to us is that He came from the heavens to the earth, and when He had grown up and come out to
minister, He went to preach the gospel place by place and
house by house. For example, He went to the house of Zaccheus (vv. 1-9) and sat beside the well in Samaria (John 4:3-7)
to visit and to wait for sinners who were chosen by God.

God Himself Coming to Visit and Seek Man

Actually, God's coming to man and visiting man in this way
did not begin when He became flesh. We know from Genesis 3
that as soon as mankind fell, when Adam and Eve sinned,
they began to fear God, turning away and hiding themselves
from the face of God. However, God did not let them go. He
did not send an angel from heaven to summon the sinners
Adam and Eve before Him, as a law court summons people
with a warrant for their arrest. God did not do that. He Himself came to the garden of Eden, the place of their fall, and
called to Adam, asking, "Where are you?" (v. 9). We can say
that the first instance of knocking on doors and paying a visit
occurred in Genesis 3 when God came to "knock on Adam's
door." Perhaps some would argue with us, saying that back
then, in the garden of Eden, houses were not yet invented, so
there were no doors to knock on. Still, I would say that in
Genesis 3 God already knocked directly on the door of man's
heart.

In Genesis 18 there is a story about a man named Abraham who lived in tents. One day when he was sitting at the entrance of his tent under the shade of the tree in the heat of the day, he suddenly saw three visitors coming to visit him. One of the visitors was Jehovah God. Actually, it was the Lord coming with two angels. This was a special visit. Abraham went forward immediately to greet them and received them eagerly, fetching water for them to wash their feet. Furthermore, Abraham prepared for them a feast of cakes and a calf. This story puzzles many Bible expositors. However, Jehovah God and the two angels did feast on the meal there. Not only God ate, but the angels also ate. Whether or not God needs to eat is not for us to decide, but Genesis 18 does tell us that God, with the two angels, ate the calf-feast prepared by Abraham and his wife (vv. 1-8).

Afterward, Jehovah stayed there for quite a while, and when He was leaving, Abraham, as an intimate friend who was reluctant to part with Him, walked with Jehovah to send Him away (v. 16). Genesis 18 recounts how Abraham touched God's heart in sending Him away. God said, "Shall I hide from Abraham what I am about to do?" (v. 17). God truly visited Abraham as a friend. The Old Testament says that God saw Abraham as His intimate friend (2 Chron. 20:7; Isa. 41:8).

Moreover, in the Old Testament we often see the expression, "The Spirit of Jehovah came upon..." (Judg. 3:10). Again and again the Spirit of Jehovah came to man, to the leaders among the children of Israel, and to all the prophets. His coming was His visiting. Actually, door-knocking is visiting. *Knocking* is a very courteous and polite term in the Chinese language. Door-knocking is visitors going to people's houses with much propriety and courtesy. Therefore, when we go out today, we do not bang on doors or trouble people, but we knock on doors and visit people.

The Lord Sending Disciples
to Seek Out the Sons of Peace

In the New Testament age the Lord Jesus came. He was the Jehovah God who sought for Adam in the garden of Eden; He was the One who visited Abraham beside the oaks of Mamre in Genesis 18; He was also the One who came upon and visited the prophets throughout the generations. Now He was not visiting man merely in His divinity or in His Godhead, but He Himself put on a body of flesh and blood, putting on our humanity and becoming even as we are, to visit man who was on the earth. On the earth He preached the gospel from place to place for three years, but not once did He send out invitations for people to come. He went to visit people Himself; He went to where they were. In His divinity and Godhead He was omnipresent, yet after He became flesh He was very much restricted by space. If He was in Galilee, He could not be in Jerusalem; if He was in Jerusalem, He could not be in Samaria. He was very much restricted by the flesh. For this reason, He sent out the twelve disciples (Luke 9:1), and later He took another step and sent seventy others (10:1).

The Lord's sending out the seventy is recorded in Luke 10, particularly in verses 1 through 6 and verse 16. In the past we did not see the light concerning visitation from house to house in this passage. In verse 3 the Lord Jesus says, "I send you as lambs in the midst of wolves." The Lord sent the disciples as lambs in the midst of wolves, so when we go out to knock on doors and visit people, do not be afraid of their rejections or their reproach. We need to be alert, because not all the people we visit are wolves; there are sons of peace among the wolves (v. 6). Today there are millions and millions of sons of Adam on this earth, but among them some are the sons of peace, who were born in the world yet chosen and predestinated by God before the foundation of the earth.

In the past we preached the gospel by the way of gospel meetings. We set up love feasts and spent much effort in inviting people to come. When they came, they felt that they were doing us a favor and "saving our faces." Sometimes they would refuse to come even when we had tried our best. This was not the way of the Lord Jesus. The Lord sent seventy people two by two to go out and visit people (v. 1) and to stay in people's houses (v. 7). Upon entering a house, they would not speak of the weather or of the world situation, but "into whatever house you enter, first say, Peace to this house" (v. 5).

They are the sons of peace, and the Lord is the Lord of peace. The Lord came to the earth to bring peace to men. When the Lord Jesus was born, the angels praised God, saying, "Glory in the highest places to God, and on earth peace among men of His good pleasure" (2:14). The men of God's good pleasure are those chosen and predestinated by God. They are the sons of peace. The Lord was born in the world to bring peace to men on the earth; He also sent out the disciples that they would go with His peace.

Furthermore, the Lord told the disciples in chapter ten verse 16, "He who hears you hears Me, and he who rejects you rejects Me, and he who rejects Me rejects Him who sent Me." This means that the Lord comes with the Father; the Lord and the Father are one, so the Lord's going is the Father's going. We also have become one with the Lord, so our going is not merely our going as representatives of the Lord, but it is also our going with the Lord; the Lord goes with us. Therefore, when we go, we bring the peace of the Lord with us; the Lord is the peace-bringer. There is a prophecy in Genesis 49, which says, "Until Shiloh comes" (v. 10). *Shiloh* means "one who brings peace." Christ came to bring peace to those whom God has chosen on the earth. Today we need to cause this peace to reach those whom God has chosen, not by inviting them to come, but by being sent to go to them. We go with peace, and this peace is the Lord Jesus. The Lord Jesus said that if the people in a house are worthy of peace, if they are chosen and predestinated by God and are men of God's good pleasure, they will surely receive us with joy and rejoicing. Otherwise, they will reject us, and this rejection is a proof that they are not the sons of peace.

Everyone of you who has gone door-knocking before has had this experience: When someone opened the door, you would often know whether or not this one was a son of peace. You could tell upon first sight that some were not the sons of peace. Why? Because the way they answered the door was like that of tigers ready to devour their prey. Not only would they reject you, they would even yell at you while sending you away. This is why when some went door-knocking, their hands would tremble and their knees would knock, deeply fearing that once the doors opened, they would be yelled at and would lose their composure. Because of this we should know that reproaches are inevitable, but they are worth it. Even the Lord Jesus was reproached by men. When we go door-knocking, we all should be prepared to be yelled at. However, we know that there will always be some sons of peace among those who open the door to us, if not one out of ten then perhaps one out of twenty; if not, then certainly one out of thirty.

Today the work of Christianity is exactly the opposite. It asks people to come instead of going to people. Although we have come out of Christianity, we are still under the influence of the poison and the atmosphere of Christianity. In the past we too have not seen this way of going out to visit people and seeking out the sons of peace. We did not see this even when we were conducting the life-study trainings. It is not until this time, during the writing of the footnotes of the Recovery Version of the New Testament, that the Lord has shown us this light from the Gospel of Luke.

Our Need to Go and Disciple All the Nations

In Matthew 28:18-19, after His death and resurrection, the Lord Jesus came into the midst of the disciples and said to them, "All authority has been given to Me in heaven and on earth." The Lord indicated that He was the Lord of heaven and earth; heaven obeyed Him, earth obeyed Him, and even all the nations obeyed Him, so now the disciples should "go." The Lord does not want people to come; He wants us, His disciples, to go. Go and do what? The Lord went on to say, "Disciple all the nations." It is a tremendous thing if we are willing to go, for we go with all authority in heaven and on earth. The context of these verses tells us very clearly that all authority has been given to Him in heaven and on earth, so we should go.

When we go to people, we should not fear their rejection. When we go, we should be full of faith, declaring to Satan, "I come with the resurrected Christ, full of His authority in heaven and on earth." Many who go out to visit people and preach the gospel testify that the ones they visited were all very submissive. Some of the ones that were visited were college professors and some had received higher education, yet they were willing to believe in the gospel when they heard the speaking of the brothers and sisters. When the brothers and sisters said, "Now you should be baptized. Please go and change," they immediately said yes and were joyfully baptized. Sometimes even we were astonished, unable to believe that they were as submissive as lambs, doing whatever we asked them to do. What is this? This is the ascended Lord being with us. His authority follows us always. This is the message of Matthew 28.

The Lord Requiring Us
to Go Forth and Bear Fruit

In the past when we read John 15, we greatly emphasized that if we abide in the Lord, the Lord will abide in us (v. 4). But we have overlooked the purpose of the abiding. The Lord said, "I am the vine; you are the branches. He who abides in Me and I in him, he bears much fruit" (v. 5). This shows that the purpose of abiding is that we would bear much fruit. Verse 2 says, "Every branch...that does not bear fruit, He takes it away." This word shows that we are the branches of the Lord Jesus, yet if we do not bear fruit, we will be cut off from Him. To be taken away is to be cut off, which means that the branch is cut off from the vine and loses all the enjoyment of the riches of the vine, no longer being supplied by the vine's life-juice. This is very serious.

Before seeing the new way, an elder in a certain locality told us that he had never brought one person to salvation in his more than ten years of being an elder. In other words, he did not bear a single fruit. How could such an unfruitful person enjoy all the supply in Christ? Nevertheless, he felt quite good about himself because the Lord was abiding in him. We dare not to pass judgment on him, but at least we know something is wrong with unfruitfulness. We all know that in order for the branch to enjoy the riches of the vine, it must be joined to the vine and express the splendor of the vine, which is to bring forth fruit.

In verse 16 the Lord Jesus said, "You did not choose Me,

but I chose you, and I set you that you should go forth and bear fruit and that your fruit should remain." In the Greek the word rendered *go* is a strong word. Regretfully, we fail to notice it when reading the Bible. We seem to not see the word *go,* as if the Lord had only assigned us to bear fruit. The Lord went on to say, "That your fruit should remain." We all know that it is not easy for a person to believe in the Lord and be saved and baptized, and it is even more difficult for him to remain. For example, one time we baptized more than a hundred new believers, and we rejoiced greatly within, but after half a year less than five out of the hundred remained. We were quite perplexed inwardly. It seemed that the fruit was not solid enough since they were lost after a short time. This was like a child dying prematurely after he is born. How could this be?

Now, in taking the new way, we have come back to the Bible to properly re-read these related verses. As a result, we see in John 15:16 that there is the word *go.* The Lord wants us to go forth and bear fruit. If we do not go, we cannot bear fruit. Going is the prerequisite for fruit-bearing. *Go* means we should go to all the nations, going to them house by house, and then our fruit should remain. We are becoming more and more clear concerning this point. When we go door-knocking, we are "going forth." Then we baptize people and establish a meeting right away in their home. This home meeting is a shelter. Establishing a home meeting in their home is to establish a shelter to cover this home, and by this the fruit remains naturally.

Today medicine is quite advanced in the United States, so much so that even a premature infant born at five or six months is able to survive. That was certainly impossible before, but now in the United States there are, in fact, such cases of successful survival. This is done by immediately placing the newborn infant in an incubator. This incubator is his shelter, which enables him to survive. Our mistake in the past was to let go of people as soon as they were baptized, like a mother who neglects her child after he is born. How can this child remain if he is born but not cared for? Therefore, we must establish a meeting in people's homes right after we have baptized them. This home meeting is an "incubator," ensuring the survival of the newborn infant. We should see this clearly.

ESTABLISHING MEETINGS IN THE HOMES
OF THE SAINTS

In our past church life, we neglected the meetings in the homes of the saints and relied mostly on the meetings in the meeting hall. This is not according to the Bible. Acts 2:42 and 46 clearly show us that on the one hand, they met in a big meeting place in the temple, and on the other hand, they gathered in the homes. Verse 46 speaks of being in homes, or "from house to house," which, if *house* is to be used as the unit, can also be "according to house." Therefore, some translations render it as "from house to house."

The contents of these meetings from house to house are first, the teaching of the apostles, which is the teaching of the truth; second, the mutual fellowship; and third, the breaking of bread and the prayers. This means that the breaking of bread was in the homes, the prayers were in the homes, the teaching of the truth was in the homes, and the mutual fellowship was in the homes. In verse 46 we are shown that they were "breaking bread from house to house." Chapter five verse 42 says, "From house to house, they did not cease teaching and announcing the gospel of Jesus as the Christ." We can see that the teaching of the truth and the preaching of the gospel can all be done in the homes.

In Acts 12 we see that Peter was persecuted and put into prison by Herod, and then prayer was being made fervently by the church to God concerning him (v. 5b). After Peter was released from the prison by the angel, he went to the house of a sister, where there was a considerable number assembled together to pray (v. 12). Putting these two verses together, we see that the fervent prayer of the church was made not in a meeting in the meeting hall but in the home of a saint, and the home was the home of a sister. All of these verses prove that the early church life was in the homes of the saints. They taught the truth, preached the gospel, fellowshipped with one another, broke bread, and prayed in the homes. Beginning from now, our church life should be absolutely according to the pattern in the Bible, following the footsteps of the early saints. After we baptize people, we should immediately establish a home meeting in their homes in order to teach them, lead them, and help them. In other words, they should learn to know the truth, preach the gospel, have mutual fellowship, and pray and break bread in the homes. In this way the saints are able to come to the full knowledge of the truth.

THE SAINTS COMING
TO THE FULL KNOWLEDGE OF THE TRUTH

Apparently, teaching the truth in home meetings where all may participate in the fellowship does not have the prevailing atmosphere of the big meetings, yet it is very practical. Big meetings are too big. Dozens, hundreds, or even thousands of people come together to listen to one person speaking, and after listening, they forget almost everything, not having much concern for what they heard. However, when we are in a home with perhaps only three or five people, everyone learns the truth together, each one focuses and pays attention, and everyone answers each other's questions. The result of learning in this way is that the truth is impressed deeply within each person. Therefore, in purpose or in result, saints can come to the full knowledge of the truth only by meeting in the homes.

Furthermore, this issues in the functioning of each saint as a member of Christ. In the big meetings one person speaks, and everyone else listens, and after listening, everyone feels good and appreciative, yet hardly anyone functions. In the past the so-called service in the church life was mostly cleaning, ushering, or making bread, as some sisters do, and preparing the cup, as some brothers do, or at the most, sharing and giving testimonies at the end of a message meeting. Actually, the supply of the members of Christ is firstly that everyone preaches the gospel, secondly that everyone teaches the truth, and thirdly that everyone helps the newly saved ones to meet in the homes. If every saint would do this, the gospel will be widely preached, the number of saved ones will increase, and the believers will be equipped with the truth practically.

The above three points are lacking in practice not merely in the denominations but also among us. Therefore, beginning from today, our church life must take this step: After a person is saved, he should be able to preach the gospel, and after a period of time he should be able to teach the truth. Then he should be able to care for other newly saved households. The purpose and result of these practices are tremendous, giving each saint the opportunity to function. If we meet only in the meeting hall, with one person speaking and everyone else listening, whether we have three hundred people or five hundred, only a few will "monopolize" the meeting, and all the other saints will have no opportunity to function. We truly hope that every brother and sister will function. Everyone must have opportunities, even an abundance of opportunities. This is our goal.

Finally, we need to see that the more we practice this, the more we love the Lord, and the more we love the Lord, the more we pursue Him. Then the result of pursuing the Lord is growth in life. In this way we are able to live out the testimony of Christ, not merely the individual Christ, but even more the corporate Christ, which is every one of us living out Christ. In other words, we are the church; all the saints become one corporate entity, and all live out Christ. Our bearing the testimony of Christ is that which the apostle John spoke of: "I John, your brother and fellow partaker in the tribulation and kingdom and endurance in Jesus...because of the word of God and the testimony of Jesus" (Rev. 1:9). When people see us, they will know that we are bearing the testimony together.

Moreover, each and every saint should come to the full knowledge of the truth, as 1 Timothy 3 says, "The house of God, which is the church of the living God, the pillar and base of the truth" (v. 15). The church should uphold the truth. We are striving toward the day in which every home has a home meeting, everyone is learning the truth, and as a result everyone is able to teach the truth. In that day we can declare to Satan, to the angels, and to mankind, "The church is the pillar and base of the truth on the earth." Therefore, on the one hand, we love Him and pursue Him, growing in life; on the other hand, we live Him and bear a good testimony for Him, having the reality of the truth.

PREACHING THE GOSPEL BY DOOR-KNOCKING AND VISITING PEOPLE YIELDING RESULTS

From the result of our practice in recent years, we can see that our training is successful. Door-knocking and visiting people is truly the best way to gain people for them to believe in the Lord. Some have baptized forty-one new ones in three and a half months. According to the statistics, more than sixty people were saved and baptized every day. This is unprecedented in the history of Taiwan. Among the more than seven thousand new believers gained, we have established over two thousand new home meetings. Originally there were four hundred home meetings in the church in Taipei, and now there are over two thousand new home meetings, so together the two categories add up to about two thousand five hundred home meetings. The two thousand new home meetings were established in the last three and a half months. This proves that this new way—door-knocking house by house, preaching the gospel, and leading people to believe in the Lord and be saved—is not only feasible but yields great results.

Success in Anything Requiring Special Skills

We all know that it is easier to succeed in something if it is done by a professional. We may use growing trees as an example. In my back yard there are two trees, an apricot tree and a peach tree. Dispositionally, I am a neat person. I like to fix and arrange things in a proper order, so one day I pruned the two trees so that they were neat and tidy, pleasing to the eye. However, one year went by and then two years, and the trees did not bear any fruit. Then a third year went by, and they still did not bear fruit. I wondered what the cause might be. I thought to myself that perhaps the soil was the problem.

There was a young sister who lived in a nearby city, whose father managed an orchard. She grew up in the orchard and knew about planting and growing fruit trees. One day when she came with others to my house, she chuckled when she saw the two trees, which were as neatly pruned as if they had gotten a haircut. She was too embarrassed to say anything, so I asked her directly, "Young sister, do you know why these two trees are fruitless?" Then she told me that I should not have pruned the trees as I did. I should not have cut the branches that were drooping downward, because the drooping branches are the fruit-bearing branches. The branches I cut off were the fruit-bearing branches, and the branches I left uncut were the unfruitful branches. I then realized that I was quite foolish, thinking myself to be very capable and feeling that my work was aesthetically pleasing. In actuality, I was entirely unprofessional. This was my personal experience.

After we started to practice door-knocking and had good results, many places responded to the report and began to do the same, but the outcome was a failure. They thought that door-knocking was just knocking on doors. How difficult could that be? How could anyone not be able to do it? Although everyone can knock on doors, no one produced any result. Actually, successful door-knocking involves many details. People let certain brothers and sisters come in when they knocked on their doors, but after they entered, it seems that it would have been better for them not to say anything, because the more they talked, the more the people resented them. Therefore, some have practiced door-knocking for a period of time but became disheartened and finally stopped. Eventually, everyone was discouraged, assuming that the new way does not work. That is not true. In actuality, door-knocking requires training.

Gospel Preaching through Door-knocking Requiring Training

Some overseas saints testified that previously they went door-knocking in their locality without any results, so they did not want to do it anymore. However, some among them came to Taiwan and received training, and after they went back, they taught the saints in their locality and began door-knocking again. The result was tremendous, so they were all very joyful. Now in a little church of only one hundred people, everyone goes door-knocking with good results. Why? It is because some trained ones went back to them and led them to practice it together. The same is true in many places; all the saints in these places have been greatly encouraged.

We have found a principle: It is difficult to succeed in anything if we rely on the natural way. Rather, we must do things according to the "professional" way in order to succeed. Door-knocking has its finer points. After a number of months of studying, we have learned a few things. When we knock on a door, if after ten seconds no one answers, we should knock and wait again; then after waiting again for half a minute, do not wait any longer. If a person opens the door, we should determine within three minutes whether or not he is a son of peace. If he is a son of peace, we should stay, but if not, we should leave right away. Sometimes a person has been a God-chosen son of peace, but when we went to knock on his door on a certain day, he was not in the right mood. He may have just fought with his wife and still had a stomach full of anger, so he could not hear our speaking to him about Jesus. Therefore, we need to observe closely; perhaps we should come again another time.

These are the principles the brothers and sisters have learned from going out in the training to knock on doors. After knocking on a door, we should decide to leave or stay within three minutes; we should lead one to pray within ten minutes and make sure he is saved; and we should lead him to be baptized within another ten minutes. In other words, we should spend no more than twenty minutes in a home. It is unsuitable to stay any longer. Our former old way supposes that the more we talk, the better it is. Actually, sometimes the more we talk, the more problems we have. During our visit we should do our best to not use our own words. It is best to use the booklet, "The Mystery of Human Life," in which are four keys that are more than adequate to meet various needs.

We must pay attention to another principle. When going out to visit people, the new trainees should not speak at first but should simply learn in a good way. Whether you are an elder, a co-worker, or an apostle, you must become an apprentice. As long as it is your first time to go out, do not speak too much, but watch and learn. An elderly brother, who is an elder, heard about this training when he came back to Taiwan at the end of last year, and one day he joined the training. He knew about this rule and was willing to abide by it. He had been in the church life for many years, so naturally he was full of knowledge and felt that he had many things to say. Moreover, seeing that the young people knew only to read a section from "The Mystery of Human Life" tempted him very much. That certainly was not easy for him. In the end, however, he too saw that door-knocking has its finer points.

One time this elderly brother went out with the door-knocking brothers and sisters, and they entered into a couple's home. Initially the wife stayed in her room and did not want to come out. A young sister spoke to the husband, and just when she felt that she had spoken enough and he was ready to be baptized, the wife came out. The young sister felt that the wife should be taken care of, and since she thought that the elderly brother should know what to do after being with them for a day, she asked him to help the husband to be baptized. Then the sister went to take care of the wife. Because of her care for the wife, the wife was baptized. However, when she turned around, the elderly brother was still talking with the husband about baptism. Right away this sister went over and talked to the husband, and after just a few words, he was also baptized. This elderly brother finally saw that door-knocking indeed requires training.

The Statistical Estimation
Regarding the Gospelization of Taiwan

Previously there were more than forty thousand baptized brothers and sisters on the island of Taiwan. With the addition of the seven thousand brought in through the trainees' door-knocking, the total comes to almost fifty thousand. Among the original forty thousand, one out of four goes to meetings regularly. Therefore, the total number of regular meeting-goers adds up to about ten thousand people, of which at least four thousand are in the church in Taipei.

With these ten thousand as the base number, if one out of twenty is a full-timer, there should be five hundred full-timers. Actually, today there are more than six hundred full-timers on the island of Taiwan. According to percentage, though, there should be five hundred full-timers per ten thousand people. According to the experiment in the training, if each of these five hundred full-timers goes door-knocking every week, five days a week and two to three hours per day, one person is guaranteed to be baptized per week. In this way, fifty-two people can be gained within a year of fifty-two weeks. If we adjust the number slightly, they can gain at least forty people. Therefore, if these five hundred full-timers each gains forty people every year, together they will gain twenty thousand.

If another two thousand five hundred go out door-knocking only once a week for two to three hours, they will each be able to gain and baptize one person per month, according to the above calculations. We may estimate that each one of them gains at least eight people per year. Two thousand five hundred multiplied by eight gives us twenty thousand people. Added to the twenty thousand gained by the full-timers, the total number of people is forty thousand. In this way, the number of people who attend meetings regularly will increase by another ten thousand, increasing from the original ten thousand to twenty thousand.

Therefore, our goal is to baptize forty thousand people on the island of Taiwan this year. In order to carry this out, we need five hundred full-timers plus two thousand five hundred who will go out door-knocking weekly. Now that I have put the burden upon you, I will no longer let you live your days in ease and comfort. We all need to strive toward this goal. If some cannot keep up, we need to urge them on. If some disagree, we need to believe that the Lord we serve has a way, and since He has begun a good work, He will complete this work Himself. If we disagree, then we have fallen behind and are not up-to-date, and in so doing we disqualify ourselves.

Being Trained in One Accord

Therefore, each one of us needs to be trained. It would be valuable if we could spare even just two nights per week. Never say lightly that anyone can go door-knocking; going door-knocking and gaining people to be baptized is not as simple as it seems. We may use playing the piano as an example. Anyone can push down the keys and make a banging sound, but no one can play a melody without adequate training. Therefore, today whether you are an elder or a co-worker, whether you are young or old, you need to be trained in a good way. There are many who have been in the church for many years who find it difficult to follow along and learn, but I am sorry to say that we have no other choice; this is our only way. Those who can take this way will keep up. Those who cannot take it have to ask the Lord for the grace to not be alienated from this way.

The Key to Success Being with the Elders

Whether or not the new way will be successful depends on the elders. Therefore, the elders must have thorough fellowship, striving together with one soul for the gospelization of Taiwan. In the past some localities did not understand our practice and wondered why training was needed. Now they all are clear that door-knocking is not as simple as it seems. The success rate of merely following the practice is quite low, and such success does not last. Success can only come out of being trained in the training and continuing steadfastly in the principle of the new way. If we spread this message quickly to the entire island and to the whole world, and everyone is able to practice accordingly, we can expect the whole world to be gospelized in the near future.

(A message given in a conference on February 1, 1987 in Taipei.)

CHAPTER EIGHT

THE NEW WAY PRODUCING THE NEW MAN, AND THE NEW MAN WALKING THE NEW WAY

THE NEW WAY—THE GOD-ORDAINED WAY

Concerning the new way, we have a saying with two simple phrases: "The new way produces the new man; the new man walks the new way." Simply speaking, the new way is to have us carry out what the Lord has commissioned. The Lord's commission to us can be divided into four main items: the gospel, the truth, life, and the church. In order to carry out these four items, we have found a most scriptural way through our more than sixty years of experience in the Lord's recovery and the practices of all the different Christian groups in the past two thousand years. This way is ordained by God and confirmed and led by the Holy Spirit, and it is a most effective way.

In the past two thousand years there were some who practiced this way, but regretfully no one took this way as the unique way. This time, in changing the system, we will take this way as the prescribed way.

Leading People to Salvation

First, we need to go door-knocking, leading people to salvation. Door-knocking is truly a very feasible way. One person among us even gained and baptized one hundred twenty people in just over two months. This is tremendous.

Leading People to Know the Truth

Second, we need to lead people to know the truth. This truth is not what is generally known—the common, superficial, and shallow truth. This truth concerns God's eternal economy, which is God in His Divine Trinity dispensing Himself into His chosen people by passing through all the processes that they may be regenerated, sanctified, transformed, conformed, and glorified, and that they may be the members of Christ and become the Body of Christ as God's corporate expression on the earth. This is the truth we are talking about.

After knocking on doors and preaching the gospel, we must go on to establish meetings in the homes of the newly baptized saints and begin to teach them the truth. This truth is the essence of the Bible, the center of the Bible, and what is according to God's heart's desire; yet this truth is mostly neglected among Christians. Some people touch only the surface of the Bible when they read the Scriptures, thus concluding that the Bible is a shallow book and contains nothing of great value. However, I have studied this book from my youth to this day, for over sixty years. The more I study the Bible, the more I have come to know its mysteries and sense deeply its utter preciousness, because this book talks about God's eternal economy.

The word *economy* is a great matter. There is in God an economy, which is to dispense Himself, by passing through all the processes, into His chosen and redeemed people, that they may be one with Him and become the Body of Christ, expressing God on the earth. Whether going out door-knocking or going to people's homes to lead the meetings, we need to learn this truth in a thorough way. Not only should we know and understand it, but we should study it to the point where we can teach others as if our tongue were the pen of a ready writer. Every newly baptized brother or sister, after attending such meetings for six months, can also become one who teaches others. In this way, many people will soon come to know the truth of the Bible. This is only a guide, to lead all the newly saved ones to read the Bible in a good way and understand all the truth in the sixty-six books of the Bible. This is the commission of the truth of which we speak.

Leading People to Grow in Life

Third, we need to lead people to grow in life. Truth brings

light, life, power, and spiritual things, comprising all the riches of God. Therefore, when we teach the truth to others, spontaneously they receive the supply of life and grow in life. The life mentioned in the Bible is the uncreated, eternal life of God. This life is neither outside of God nor apart from God; this life is God Himself. In other words, this life is the Spirit, and the Spirit is Christ. Therefore, when we minister life to others, we minister the Spirit to them, and we minister Christ to them.

The eternal life is the Spirit and it is also Christ. Today we have all received this life. Hymn #377 in the Chinese *Hymns* says, "Glory! Glory! Christ my life to be; / Glory! Glory! The Spirit leadeth me." However, we cannot stop here. We need to see that the purpose of God's imparting His life to us is that we may be regenerated, transformed, and conformed to the image of His Son and become His church, His golden lampstands which appear in every place, shining on and enlightening the world.

Raising Up Churches

Fourth, we must raise up the ones who have been baptized, edified in the truth, and have grown in life to be the church. Generally, people see Christianity as a religion. However, in the Bible *religion* is not a positive term (Acts 26:5); it is a negative term. In other words, the Bible depreciates religion. In that case, is the so-called Christianity a religion or not? This must be viewed from two perspectives. The Christianity that is orthodox and scriptural is not a religion. Although people attach "-anity" to it, in reality the Bible does not reveal a religion; it reveals Christ. According to the Bible, we believe in Christ, not Christianity.

This Christ is a living person. He is the embodiment of the Triune God—the Father, the Son, and the Holy Spirit. Today He has passed through death and resurrection and has become the all-inclusive life-giving Spirit, so we can breathe Him and be filled and occupied with Him. When we meet, He is with us, and He operates in the meeting in various ways, giving grace to every brother and sister. This is the Christ we preach, believe in, worship, and serve. We are not a religion, nor are we the so-called Christianity. We are a group of people who enjoy Christ and serve Christ together.

From another perspective, according to its transmuted condition, Christianity is truly a great religion. The biggest party in Christianity is Catholicism, followed by Protestantism. Within Protestantism are many sects and denominations as well. We do not represent such Christianity; we represent the church of God. This church is the living Body of Christ, constituted of all who have the eternal life of God. In order to carry out these four main items—the gospel, the truth, life, and the church—we have to rely on the Holy Spirit and the words of the Bible, with much prayer and redoubled diligence and labor. Then again, these things are very general. We see that the results of our more than sixty years of experience, in addition to the practices of all the different groups in Christianity in the past two thousand years, are indeed unsatisfactory. In order to carry out these four main items today practically, each one of us must practice door-knocking, visiting people, preaching the gospel, and going to people's homes to teach the truth and minister life.

THE SPECIFIC PRACTICE OF THE NEW WAY

Producing One Full-timer out of Every Twenty People

None of these matters—door-knocking, visiting people, teaching the truth, and ministering life—are simple. Bringing people into the Body of Christ to live the church life is even more difficult. All of these things need time and manpower. Therefore, after repeated study and consultation with various sources and with much prayer, we deeply felt that in order to carry out these four main items, we need to produce one full-timer out of every twenty people from among those who meet.

Currently the church in Taipei has over ten thousand names on the list, but there are only four thousand regular meeting-goers. From among these four thousand, we should be able to produce two hundred full-time serving ones. One full-timer should be produced out of every twenty people, and the other nineteen should endeavor to support this one.

According to our observations and experiences, we believe that since all the full-timers spend most of their time meeting on the Lord's Day, they do not have to go door-knocking on that day, but they should go door-knocking every day of the rest of the week. For these six days, they do not need to go door-knocking eight hours each day. They need to go simply for about one-third of eight hours, two and a half hours or three hours at the most. Six consecutive days of door-knocking per week would guarantee one person being gained and baptized every week. In this way, a full-timer's labor will be able to bring in fifty-two people through door-knocking during the fifty-two weeks of the year, and two hundred full-timers will be able bring in ten thousand four hundred people, which rounded down is ten thousand people.

One out of Every Four People
Going Door-knocking Every Week

Next, one out of every four people who meet regularly should go out at least once a week to knock on doors, visit people, teach the truth, or fellowship with people and minister life to them, each for two hours. Four thousand people meet in the church in Taipei, so there can be one thousand part-time serving ones going door-knocking every week. To be sure, door-knocking in this way every week for two hours, at least one person will be saved every two months, or every eight weeks. In a conservative estimation one person can gain six people per year; one thousand can gain six thousand. This, added to the people gained by the two hundred full-timers, gives us sixteen thousand people, which is the quadruple of four thousand. This requires us to carry it out together.

"Rescue the perishing, / Care for the dying, / Snatch them in pity from sin and the grave; / Weep o'er the erring one, / Lift up the fallen, / Tell them of Jesus the mighty to save. / Rescue the perishing, / Care for the dying; / Jesus is merciful, / Jesus will save" (Hymns, #921, stanza 1 and chorus). The elders should take the lead to rescue the perishing. From now on, the elders will not sit in the offices in the meeting halls, but they will go door-knocking every day. One experience of door-knocking is different from another; there is little value when a careless person goes door-knocking, but there is much value when a dignified and noble person goes door-knocking. Therefore, it is weightier when the elders go door-knocking. According to what the Bible says, elders should not be "as lording it over your allotments but by becoming patterns of the flock" (1 Pet. 5:3). To this end, the elders should be the first to go door-knocking to be the patterns of the flock.

If every twenty people produce one full-timer and every four people produce one who goes door-knocking weekly, then with four thousand people as the base number, Taipei will be able to gain sixteen thousand people in a year through door-knocking—a fourfold multiplication. If we continue in this way, Taipei will have gained two million seven hundred thousand through door-knocking by 1990. Let us wait and see, but please do not be a bystander. Every twenty saints produce one full-timer; every four produce one part-timer; the elders take the lead in preaching the gospel; and all the saints pray with one accord and endeavor to provide financially. If we do this, the Lord will have a way.

I firmly believe that the gospelization of Taiwan can be fulfilled in five years under the leading of the grace of the Lord. According to various observations and general experiences, we do have the full assurance that we can gospelize the whole of Taiwan. Therefore, we have to pray for the gospelization of Taiwan within five years. Starting from January of next year, the four hundred fifty full-timers will begin to move on this island. There are two hundred fifty from overseas in this term of the training. Out of these two hundred fifty, one hundred eighteen signed a petition requesting me to allow them to stay in Taiwan for at least a year. Some even requested to stay until Taiwan is fully gospelized. It would also be effective if only the native saints went door-knocking, yet it would definitely be more effective if every team included a foreigner, especially an American. Sometimes the same words are not as easily received when they are spoken by a Chinese person as when they are spoken by a foreigner.

Therefore, the gospelization, truth-ization, and churchization of Taiwan in five years is a promising prospect. I hope the saints in all the churches in different localities would say amen from deep within to the Lord's new move today and cooperate through prayer, with no one dissenting or speaking something different. Thank and praise the Lord that He gave us a unique way that succeeds into eternity!

(A message given in a conference on November 23, 1986 in Taipei.)

CHAPTER NINE

THE RECOVERY OF EVERYONE FUNCTIONING

THE PRACTICE OF ONLY GIVING MESSAGES KILLING THE FUNCTION OF THE SAINTS

Some of us have been listening to messages in the church for more than thirty years. How do we feel? Are we numb and without any feeling, are we very satisfied, or do we sense a lack and grieve because of it? A few decades have gone by, and we have been listening to messages, going to trainings, and participating in certain services, yet if the Lord comes back today, are we able to settle accounts with Him? What sort of account can we hand over?

Because I have worked in Taiwan for many years, the saints have given me the ground to speak, and so I speak: Taiwan pains me the most. Since 1980, I have observed that the condition of the churches in Taiwan is at a standstill, and even going backward. More than sixty years ago we came out of the denominations in China, and over thirty years ago we started the Lord's work in Taiwan. However, up until four years ago, we completely had gone back to the old ways.

We all know that Christianity gathers a group of people for a church service. They hire a speaker who has theological knowledge, who is very eloquent and capable, and who is able to run an organization and bring people together. Such persons are rare in Taiwan but quite common in the United States. They are all well-known persons in Christianity, but the work of these well-known persons has "killed" every one of their church members. On the one hand, these church members have been brought to the Lord through them, but on the other hand, their speaking has "killed" these church members. Some may say that *kill* is too strong an expression,

but at least we can say that the members have become accus-
tomed to listening to messages; they have been drugged and
become numb. They only know that a Christian should be a
proper and good person and that he should attend the church
service every Lord's Day; that is good enough. However, from
the perspective of the spiritual supply of life, such a way completely annuls the members' function.

The Bible says that all who are saved and regenerated
have been transferred out of Adam and into Christ; they are
all members of the Body of Christ. Moreover, each member of
this Body has his function and should function (Rom. 12:4;
1 Cor. 12:14-22). Let us use our physical body as an example.
When we talk or move, even the little finger and the ear function, because when we talk, we do it as living persons with
lively gestures. In the same way, since we are members of the
Body of Christ, we should function in the church. However,
the functions of the fellow believers in Christianity have been
nullified by the preachers and replaced with the clergy. It is
the same for us. Very often it is only the responsible brothers
who speak in the meetings. This practice utterly kills the
saints. The more the responsible brothers speak, the less the
saints need to function and the more they lose their function.

If in a meeting only a few speak and speak too much, that
is the practice of the clergy. As for the ones listening to messages, the more they listen, the more they are drugged and
lose their function. Every week when they attend the service
they are injected with a shot of anesthetic. There are fifty-
two weeks in a year, which means fifty-two shots of anesthetic per year. After a whole year, will they have any feeling
left? They will be only dumb and ignorant.

The saddest thing is that some saints, who were very
lively in the beginning, after listening to messages for over
thirty years have gradually lost their function, as if they no
longer have any feeling. The Bible tells us that we live in
expectation of the Lord's coming. In Matthew 25, after the
Lord told the parable of the ten virgins going forth to meet
the bridegroom (vv. 1-13), He also told a parable of the slaves
receiving talents (vv. 14-30). This means that when the Lord
comes again, not only will we go forth to see His face, but we

also will hand over our account to Him. Therefore, we need to work for the Lord; we need to serve Him. If we do not work and do not serve the Lord, when He comes, we will be unable to hand over our account.

The slave who received one talent hid all of it in the earth. He said to the master, "Behold, you have what is yours" (v. 25). But the master immediately rebuked him and said that he was an "evil and slothful slave" (v. 26). Apparently, the slave did not do anything wrong, yet he did not use the possessions the master gave him to do business or accumulate interest. In other words, he did not bear fruit. Therefore, the master rebuked him. We are sad and in pain because many saints have lost all their function, not after listening to messages for thirty years in the denominations, but after listening to messages for thirty years among us. All of them were born, grew up, and received spiritual education in the Lord's recovery, and they also pursued the books in the Lord's recovery, but the result has been no different from being in the denominations. How can we listen to messages under the same roof for thirty years and still remain exactly the same as we were thirty years ago? What excuse do we have?

This is why we say repeatedly that the way of Christianity is terrible. One person speaking and everyone else listening only kills us and numbs us and causes us to lose our function. Not only Christianity but all religions restrict people. A school textbook defines religion in this way: "Religion circumscribes the heart of man." Religion is used to regulate man. Therefore, the benefit of Christianity is that due to one's belief in this religion, he observes all the rules and regulations and no longer does bad things. Nowadays we seem to have fallen into such a condition. Ordinarily we follow the rules and regulations, and on the Lord's Day we attend the church service. However, this causes us to lose our function and feeling. This is Christianity; this is religion.

Our more than thirty years of work in Taiwan is now in such a state. How can we not be in pain? It was not like this when we first began to work in Taiwan. Then we were full of vigor, and the saints all functioned. Hence, there was a thirtyfold increase at the end of the year. The first year yielded a thirtyfold increase, and after the fourth or the fifth year we had a hundredfold increase. Within just a few years, the number multiplied from a few hundred to tens of thousands. There were joint meetings, meetings according to halls, meetings according to groups within the halls, and meetings under the leading ones within the groups. However, by 1980 in every church only the few good speakers spoke. For example, Taipei plainly had ten to twenty thousand saints but only four or five elders. How was it that no one else could be an elder? That is why in 1984, when I went back to Taiwan to change the system, more than eighty elders were added. We cannot have the practice of religious hierarchy, annulling the opportunity for the saints to function. For the increase of the church, we need to help every saint to function.

I certainly have an indignation welling up within me because Taiwan has shown no progress. Since the churches in Taiwan were produced through my service, I will save the politeness and be blunt. However, this is not a matter of being polite or of keeping a good relationship, nor is it a matter of saving their face. If I cared for these things, I would not be here doing the Lord's work. I abandoned my own career and my own life for the Lord's work. I am not speaking words of conceit; I would have had success even if I did not love the Lord and had pursued a career in the world instead. However, that is not what I want. What I want is for the Lord's recovery to be on the earth.

Taiwan is in such a condition, and it is the same in the United States. I have told the responsible brothers in the United States that this situation is altogether wrong. This forced me to return to Taiwan, to reconsider the entire situation, to reconsider the way to meet in the Bible, and to re-examine the practices of all the groups in Christian history. I have even studied the existing denominations, as well as Mormonism and Jehovah's Witness, and even the way people do business in the world. As a result, the Lord opened my eyes and showed me that I need to completely abandon all of Christianity's ways. Not only should we come out of Christianity, but we should also abandon everything of Christianity. Whatever is of Christianity as a religion we cannot have and we do not want.

THE WAY OF HOME MEETINGS AND VISITING PEOPLE

I sought before the Lord, what should we do if we do not take the way of Christianity? The Lord then showed me that, first, the church life is not in the big meetings. In the early days of the church, the church life was in the homes (Acts 2:46), such as the church in the home of Aquila and Priscilla. The New Testament mentions at least three or four homes in which there was a church (Rom. 16:5; 1 Cor. 16:19; Col. 4:15; Philem. 2), but it does not speak of a church in a large gathering. Therefore, we see the importance of homes. Second, the Lord showed me that the very basis of the way to carry out His salvation is to go out and visit people. The Lord Himself took the first step, leaving the throne in the heavens to come to the earth to visit man. During His three and a half years of work, He always went to visit people, yet not once did He invite people to come and listen to messages. He went to the house of Zaccheus (Luke 19:1-10), and He went beside the well in Samaria (John 4:1-8). He went and visited people. Through this, my eyes were opened, and I saw the errors of the past. In the past we exhausted much effort yet rarely produced a single fruit. Even if we gained one person, we could not hold on to him. This was our condition in the past.

The statistics of Christianity in the twenty-two years from 1964 to 1986 further confirmed my feeling: the way of Christianity does not work. Of the five major denominations, four have been decreasing in number drastically. Only one has stayed above water, but its rate of increase is a mere 1.48 percent. I have studied several historical events. After Martin Luther brought in the Reformation, the Mystics of the 1600s were greatly revered by people, but over time they seem to have vanished without a trace. The Brethren were the same. They brought in many truths to Christianity, thriving and flourishing for a time, but today they also have become desolate, with only ninety-eight thousand members in the entire United States. This is hard for me to believe. Likewise, the inner-life group, that Austin-Sparks was with, no longer has much influence.

Therefore, I arrived at the conclusion that the way practiced in the Bible is the only proper way, the unique way. The Bible tells us to "go"—to go and visit people, to go and disciple all the nations. The word *go* is found in John 15:16. The Lord said, "I chose you, and I set you that you should go forth and bear fruit." If we do not go, we cannot bear fruit. This "going" is what we call door-knocking, which is to go and knock on doors to visit people. Door-knocking is for visiting people.

However, this going involves very many details. Most importantly, we go for the accomplishing of God's selection and predestination. Before the foundation of the world, God chose and predestinated a number of people among mankind. Who is able to go and seek out these people? The Lord Jesus was the first to answer God's calling. He came to the world to seek the lost. He sought out those whom God chose and predestinated. Next, He sent forth the twelve disciples two by two and charged them, saying, "I send you forth as sheep in the midst of wolves" (Matt. 10:16). The wonderful thing is that there are sons of peace among the wolves (Luke 10:6). In the Lord's eyes, today's society is like a pack of wolves. When we go, however, we need only be concerned with going house by house, because there will be the sons of peace. Regardless of which house we go into, if someone believes, he is one chosen and predestinated by God before the foundation of the world; he is a son of peace. Even though he is among the wolves, he is a son of peace. Today there are millions of wolves in the world, but at least some among them are the sons of peace. We must go to them and bring them back.

DOOR-KNOCKING AND VISITING PEOPLE
TO SEEK OUT THE SONS OF PEACE

When we go door-knocking, we should make sure that we are not discouraged by people's not opening their doors or by their rejection after they open their doors. Someone gave this kind of testimony. A certain brother went door-knocking, but no one received him. However, he was not discouraged; he told his companions to go back, and he continued to knock on doors by himself. He said, "I will not quit today until I get one person to be baptized." In the end, he baptized someone in a home. There was indeed a son of peace among the wolves. We should believe that in the world there are sons of peace, ones chosen by God. We owe it to them to go visit them and lead them to salvation. Therefore, we need to "go," going door-knocking and visiting people to seek out the sons of peace.

We have knocked on one hundred thousand doors in four months. We have found out that the faster the door-knocking is, the better. Once someone opens the door, we should know whether or not he is a son of peace. If not, we should politely say good-bye and quickly go to the next door. If we run into a quarreling couple, we should understand that they will not be receptive for the time; we should leave quickly and come back after two weeks. After we knock on the door and go in, we should give people only a taste and not linger for more than twenty minutes. We should lead them to believe within three to five minutes, lead them to prayer within ten minutes, and help them to be baptized within fifteen minutes. In this way, we can leave within twenty minutes. There is no need for more conversation. Although some people welcome us, once they start talking, they go on without end. The conversation goes from Confucius and Mencius to the current world situation, and two hours go by, but in the end they have not reached a conclusion. This is a waste of time. Door-knocking is not very simple.

Door-knocking is effective because, firstly, it is according to God's will. Secondly, it is because we are carrying it out in a way that is altogether new from the inside out. From the time we began to meet in Chefoo, we often studied this matter without discovering its secret. After seeking for many years, we have truly seen through the way of Christianity, realizing that we should never take the way of one person speaking and everyone else listening. In the past, however, we have mostly adopted the way of Christianity. Although we tried to keep the good and get rid of the bad, we did not change altogether from the inside out. This time, we are truly changing altogether from the inside out. By changing the system, we have discarded the poor tradition of one person speaking and everyone else listening, and we are no longer waiting in the meeting halls and inviting people to come; rather, we are going door-knocking house by house.

In Matthew 28 the Lord Jesus said, "Go therefore and disciple all the nations" (v. 19). In Acts 1 He said, "You shall be My witnesses both in Jerusalem and in all Judea and Samaria and unto the uttermost part of the earth" (v. 8). Therefore, we need to knock on every door in the whole world, seeking out the sons of peace one by one from among the wolves. Thus, we will be able to hand over our account when we see the Lord.

BAPTIZING PEOPLE AND SETTING UP HOME MEETINGS

The training in door-knocking and gospel preaching in Taipei is very strict, with definite principles guiding our timing and the content of our speaking. For example, we can leave if the door is not opened within half a minute after knocking. Also, we all should use the gospel booklet "The Mystery of Human Life." This booklet always hits the mark in preaching the gospel. As for baptism, our practice in the past was to wait after someone was saved until the following week to have a baptism interview with him, and only then baptize him. We can compare baptism to the way sisters stir-fry vegetables. The timing and the control of temperature are very crucial; once you miss the right temperature, the vegetables will not turn out well even if you try to fry them again. The baptisms in the past were too formal. To wait for a week to baptize someone after he believes in the Lord and after he has a baptism interview, is too formal. Baptism is the first step of man's salvation that he needs to take after he believes, because "he who believes and is baptized shall be saved" (Mark 16:16). Moreover, when we baptize people, we baptize them into the Triune God. This is the first thing the Lord wants us to do.

The second thing is to establish home meetings, which is for bearing remaining fruit. In the past, whether in Taiwan or in the United States, the fruit we bore rarely remained. Sometimes we baptized more than ten people, yet we could not keep even one of them. This is like a mother, who after giving birth to seven children, cannot keep even one of them alive. Why is this? It is because they are not cared for. After we baptize people, if we do not look after them and feed them, it is the same as begetting children but not caring for them. This is why the newly saved ones never remained.

In practicing the new way, the Lord has shown us that right after baptizing people we should invite them to establish a home meeting. To establish a home meeting is to establish a protection, not only to protect the new ones, but also to protect ourselves. Then we should go back and visit them in two days. There is no mother who does not love her child when she sees him. We all love whom we beget, and we are willing to go and see them repeatedly; the more we see them, the more we want to see them. Therefore, this is a mutual safeguard between us and the new ones. We meet with them in their homes in a very normal way; this is the meeting of the church. How sweet it is when we lead the new ones to break bread and pray together!

In this way, none of the brothers and sisters will be idle. We truly desire to open a way that all may go out door-knocking. After knocking on doors, we bring people to believe and be baptized, and then we establish meetings in the homes of all the new ones. After we have baptized a person in this way, this person becomes a child begotten by us, so we must go and visit him. When we go visit him, even if there is nothing to say, even if we go only to see him, he is still cherished. When a mother has given birth to a child, although the child is not able to speak yet, the mother still plays with him and speaks to him, and in so doing she cherishes the child. Our care for the new ones should be the same.

DOOR-KNOCKING, HOME MEETINGS, AND EVERYONE FUNCTIONING

It is not easy when we first go out door-knocking, but one day, when a person is baptized, this new one will stir us up. After two days, we will go and visit him again, and he will become our responsibility. If this continues, one after another, every one of us will have something to do.

A few days after their baptism, some may want to go door-knocking with us and learn how to preach the gospel. We should then take them through the entire course, going out together to baptize people and to meet, teach the truth, and supply life in the new one's homes. After a few months they will be able to do so accordingly. In this way all the saints are put into action, each fulfilling his duty, and the clergy system naturally ceases to exist.

However, in order for there to be fellowship among the saints, we can have a gathering of the entire assembly every two months. Perhaps on the first Lord's Day of every month the whole church can gather together for the breaking of bread, for some messages, and for some fellowship so that the saints may know one another and all may be encouraged.

This way of door-knocking and visiting people to preach the gospel and establish meetings in their homes is absolutely the right way. May all of us practice it. From now on there will not be only the speaking of the elders and co-workers in the churches, which annuls the functions of the saints. That is the old way; that is not meeting in the new way. We all should go out door-knocking to establish meetings one by one in this way. If someone is saved through door-knocking, we should establish a meeting in his home. If another one is saved through door-knocking, we should also establish a meeting in his home. If these two homes are close to each other, after two or three weeks they can have a joint meeting so that they can get to know one another.

In the past our meetings were full of old stories, and after meeting for a few decades we still talked about the same old things. Eventually, we lost our taste and excitement for the meetings; all we saw were the same old faces. The meeting in the practice of the new way does not have idle talk and does not pass the time in boredom. Rather, the meetings are with mutual questioning and answering, all learning the truth together. This is the way we should take today.

(A message given in the Lord's table meeting on January 18, 1987 in Anaheim.)

ABOUT THE AUTHOR

Witness Lee was born in 1905 in northern China and raised in a Christian family. At age 19 he was fully captured for Christ and immediately consecrated himself to preach the gospel for the rest of his life. Early in his service, he met Watchman Nee, a renowned preacher, teacher, and writer. Witness Lee labored together with Watchman Nee under his direction. In 1934 Watchman Nee entrusted Witness Lee with the responsibility for his publication operation, called the Shanghai Gospel Bookroom.

Prior to the Communist takeover in 1949, Witness Lee was sent by Watchman Nee and his other co-workers to Taiwan to ensure that the things delivered to them by the Lord would not be lost. Watchman Nee instructed Witness Lee to continue the former's publishing operation abroad as the Taiwan Gospel Bookroom, which has been publicly recognized as the publisher of Watchman Nee's works outside China. Witness Lee's work in Taiwan manifested the Lord's abundant blessing. From a mere 350 believers, newly fled from the mainland, the churches in Taiwan grew to 20,000 in five years.

In 1962 Witness Lee felt led of the Lord to come to the United States, settling in California. During his 35 years of service in the U.S., he ministered in weekly meetings and weekend conferences, delivering several thousand spoken messages. Much of his speaking has since been published as over 400 titles. Many of these have been translated into over fourteen languages. He gave his last public conference in February 1997 at the age of 91.

He leaves behind a prolific presentation of the truth in the Bible. His major work, *Life-study of the Bible,* comprises over 25,000 pages of commentary on every book of the Bible from the perspective of the believers' enjoyment and experience of God's divine life in Christ through the Holy Spirit. Witness Lee was the chief editor of a new translation of the New Testament into Chinese called the Recovery Version and directed the translation of the same into English. The Recovery Version also appears in a number of other languages. He provided an extensive body of footnotes, outlines, and spiritual cross references. A radio broadcast of his messages can be heard on Christian radio stations in the United States. In 1965 Witness Lee founded Living Stream Ministry, a non-profit corporation, located in Anaheim, California, which officially presents his and Watchman Nee's ministry.

Witness Lee's ministry emphasizes the experience of Christ as life and the practical oneness of the believers as the Body of Christ. Stressing the importance of attending to both these matters, he led the churches under his care to grow in Christian life and function. He was unbending in his conviction that God's goal is not narrow sectarianism but the Body of Christ. In time, believers began to meet simply as the church in their localities in response to this conviction. In recent years a number of new churches have been raised up in Russia and in many eastern European countries.

OTHER BOOKS PUBLISHED BY
Living Stream Ministry

Titles by Witness Lee:

Abraham—Called by God	0-7363-0359-6
The Experience of Life	0-87083-417-7
The Knowledge of Life	0-87083-419-3
The Tree of Life	0-87083-300-6
The Economy of God	0-87083-415-0
The Divine Economy	0-87083-268-9
God's New Testament Economy	0-87083-199-2
The World Situation and God's Move	0-87083-092-9
Christ vs. Religion	0-87083-010-4
The All-inclusive Christ	0-87083-020-1
Gospel Outlines	0-87083-039-2
Character	0-87083-322-7
The Secret of Experiencing Christ	0-87083-227-1
The Life and Way for the Practice of the Church Life	0-87083-785-0
The Basic Revelation in the Holy Scriptures	0-87083-105-4
The Crucial Revelation of Life in the Scriptures	0-87083-372-3
The Spirit with Our Spirit	0-87083-798-2
Christ as the Reality	0-87083-047-3
The Central Line of the Divine Revelation	0-87083-960-8
The Full Knowledge of the Word of God	0-87083-289-1
Watchman Nee—A Seer of the Divine Revelation ...	0-87083-625-0

Titles by Watchman Nee:

How to Study the Bible	0-7363-0407-X
God's Overcomers	0-7363-0433-9
The New Covenant	0-7363-0088-0
The Spiritual Man 3 volumes	0-7363-0269-7
Authority and Submission	0-7363-0185-2
The Overcoming Life	1-57593-817-0
The Glorious Church	0-87083-745-1
The Prayer Ministry of the Church	0-87083-860-1
The Breaking of the Outer Man and the Release ...	1-57593-955-X
The Mystery of Christ	1-57593-954-1
The God of Abraham, Isaac, and Jacob	0-87083-932-2
The Song of Songs	0-87083-872-5
The Gospel of God 2 volumes	1-57593-953-3
The Normal Christian Church Life	0-87083-027-9
The Character of the Lord's Worker	1-57593-322-5
The Normal Christian Faith	0-87083-748-6
Watchman Nee's Testimony	0-87083-051-1

Available at
Christian bookstores, or contact Living Stream Ministry
2431 W. La Palma Ave. • Anaheim, CA 92801
1-800-549-5164 • www.livingstream.com